Gateway To Python Programming

Author
RAVISH BAPNA
M. Tech. (Geoinformatics)
Indian Institute of Technology Kanpur (India)

ISBN-10: 1497422019
ISBN-13: 978-1497422018

First edition: March 2014.

Publisher: Self-published.
Printed by: CreateSpace Independent Publishing Platform.

Dedicated to my grandmother
Late Smt. Ghisi Bai Bapna

PREFACE

In student community, it is still a common practice to start learning programming language with relatively harder options, such as C, C++, or Java. These languages present additional complexity that the student needs to master, which in turn slows the pace of the course. To boost the confidence level of students for learning computer programming language, it is a wise approach to choose easy path of Python programming. Students may be better served by learning Python as their first programming language because it has simple syntax, and an extensive standard library to accomplish numerous tasks. Learning Python in beginner's programming course let students concentrate on important programming skills such as problem decomposition. Python has an interactive interpreter which enables students to test language features while programming.

One can find lots of learning material for Python programming (including official documentation available at *www.python.org/*) on internet, but this book encompasses systematically compiled elementary topics to curtail exhaustive searching time. This book is also helpful even to those students who have no prior knowledge of computer programming.

I would like to express my gratitude to my parents who have motivated me to write this book. This book is outcome of above views and humbly presented for reference and studies.

Author
Ravish Bapna
E-mail address: ravish.bapna@gmail.com

ERRATA

Every effort has been made in the preparation of this book, ensuring the accuracy of the provided information. However, if any mistake is found out in this book, be it in text or code, please bring it to the notice of the author for correction. Author will be grateful for positive suggestions and corrections, if e-mailed at *ravish.bapna@gmail.com*.

The information contained in this book is sold without warranty, either express or implied. Neither the author, nor publisher, and its dealers and distributors will be held liable in any way for any damage, if caused or alleged to be caused directly or indirectly.

CONVENTION

The following convention is used in this book:
- Running text is written in Calibri font.
- Website links and other important information are highlighted with *italics* font style.
- Programs (including variables, constants etc.) are of `Courier New` font.
- Headings are of **bold** font style.

LIST OF CHAPTER CONTENTS

LIST OF ILLUSTRATIONS

LIST OF TABLES

ABBREVIATIONS

Abbreviation	Full form
ASCII	American Standard Code for Information Interchange.
BSD license	Berkeley Source Distribution license.
DOS	Disk Operating System.
GNU	GNU's Not Unix.
GNU GPL	GNU General Public License.
GUI	Graphical User Interface.
HTML	HyperText Markup Language.
MS	Microsoft.
PDF	Portable Document Format.

Chapter 1
INTRODUCTION

In this age of computers, many people use this powerful machine to try to solve variety of analytical problems, manage huge amount of data etc., and to carry out various other hectic tasks. The advancement of computer technology has resulted in development of sophisticated softwares, which culminated in reduced human effort and human involvement in numerous works. Many softwares are generally very costly and usually focus on carrying out generic tasks. But there are times when there is need to accomplish a non-generic or customized task. Such custom exercise could be entertained by writing a program using a programming language.

A programming language is an artificial language designed to communicate instructions to a machine, usually computer. Programming language is used to create programs (i.e. set of instructions) that control the behavior of a machine and/or to express algorithms precisely. Programming languages uses the same general principles, so after learning any one language, it is easy to grasp another.

1.1. Open source software

Before stepping into the world of programming using open source tools, one should try to understand the definition of open source software given by "Open Source Initiative" (abbreviated as OSI). OSI is a non-profit corporation with global scope, formed to educate about and advocate the benefits of open source software, and to build bridges among different constituencies in the open source community.

Open source software is a defined as software whose source code is made available under a license that allow modification and re-distribution of the software at will. Sometimes a distinction is made between open source software and free software as given by GNU (*http://www.gnu.org/*). The detailed distribution terms of open source software given by OSI is given on website link: *http://opensource.org/*.

1.2. Python

Python is a high-level general purpose programming language that is used in a wide variety of application domains. Python has the right combination of performance and features that demystify program writing. Some of the features of Python are listed below:
- It is a simple and easy to learn.
- Python implementation is under an open source license that makes it freely usable and distributable, even for commercial use.
- It works on many platforms such as Windows, Linux, etc.
- It is an interpreted language.
- It is an object-oriented language.
- Embeddable within applications as a scripting interface.
- Python has a comprehensive set of packages to accomplish various tasks.

Python is an interpreted language, as opposed to a compiled one, though the distinction is blurry because of the presence of the bytecode compiler (beyond the scope of this book). Python source code is compiled into bytecode, so that executing the same file is faster the second time (recompilation from source to bytecode can be avoided). Interpreted languages typically have a shorter development/debug cycle than compiled ones, and also their programs generally also run slowly. Please note that, Python uses 7-bit ASCII character set for program text.

The latest stable releases can always be found on the Python's website (*http://www.python.org/*). There are two recommended production-ready Python versions at this point in time, because at the moment there are two branches of stable releases: 2.x and 3.x. Python 3.x may be less useful than 2.x, since currently there are more third party softwares available for Python 2 than for Python 3. Python 2 code will generally not run unchanged in Python 3. This book focuses on Python version 2.7.6.

Python follows modular programming approach, which is a software design technique that emphasizes separating the functionality of a program into independent, inter-changeable modules, such that each contains everything necessary to execute only one aspect of the desired functionality. Conceptually, modules represent a separation of concerns, and improve maintainability by enforcing logical boundaries between components. More information on module is provided in chapter 5.

Python versions are numbered in the format *A.B.C* or *A.B*, where *A* is the major version number, and it is only incremented for major changes in the language; *B* is the minor version number, and incremented for relatively lesser changes; *C* is the micro-level, and it is incremented for bug-fixed release.

1.2.1. Pythonic

"Pythonic" is a bit different idea/approach of writing program, which is usually not followed in other programming languages. For example, to loop all elements of an iterable using `for` statement, usually the following approach is followed:

```
food=['pizza','burger','noodles']
for i in range(len(food)):
    print(food[i])
```

A cleaner Pythonic approach is:

```
food=['pizza','burger','noodles']
for piece in food:
    print(piece)
```

1.2.2. History

Python was created in the early 1990s by Guido van Rossum at Centrum Wiskunde & Informatica (CWI, refer *http://www.cwi.nl/*) in the Netherlands as a successor of a language called "ABC". Guido remains Python's principal author, although it includes many contributions from others. When he began implementing Python, Guido van Rossum was also reading the published scripts from "Monty Python's Flying Circus", a BBC comedy series from the 1970s. Van Rossum thought he needed a name that was short, unique, and slightly mysterious, so he decided to call the language "Python". In 1995, Guido continued his work on Python at the Corporation for National Research Initiatives (CNRI, visit *http://www.cnri.reston.va.us/*) in Reston, Virginia, where he released several versions of the software. In May 2000, Guido and the Python core development team moved to "BeOpen.com" to form the

BeOpen PythonLabs team. In October of the same year, the PythonLabs team moved to Digital Creations (now Zope Corporation, visit *http://www.zope.com/*). In 2001, the Python Software Foundation (PSF, refer *http://www.python.org/psf/*) was formed, a non-profit organization created specifically to own Python-related intellectual property. Zope Corporation is a sponsoring member of the PSF.

1.2.3. Documentation

Official Python 2.7.6 documentation can be accessed from website link: *http://docs.python.org/2/*. To download an archive containing all the documents for version 2.7.6 of Python in one of various formats (plain text, PDF, HTML), follow the link: *http://docs.python.org/2/download.html*.

1.3. Integrated development environment

An Integrated Development Environment (IDE) is an application that provides comprehensive facilities for software development. An IDE normally consists of a source code editor, compiler and/or interpreter, and a debugger.

1.3.1. IDLE

IDLE is an IDE, and it is the basic editor and interpreter environment which ships with the standard distribution of Python. IDLE is the built using "Tkinter" GUI toolkit, and has the following features:
- Coded in Python, using the Tkinter GUI toolkit.
- Cross-platform i.e. works on Windows and Unix.
- Has source code editor with multiple undo, text highlighting, smart indent, call tips and many other features (shown in figure 1-2).
- Has Python shell window, also known as "interactive interpreter" (shown in figure 1-1).

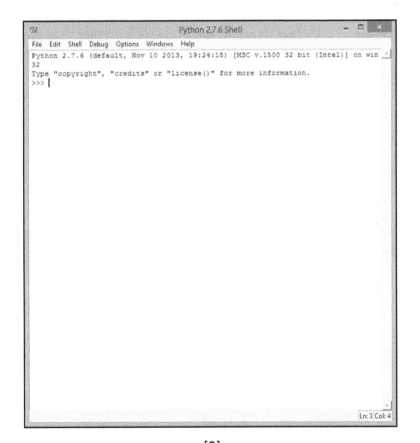

Figure 1-1: IDLE's Python shell

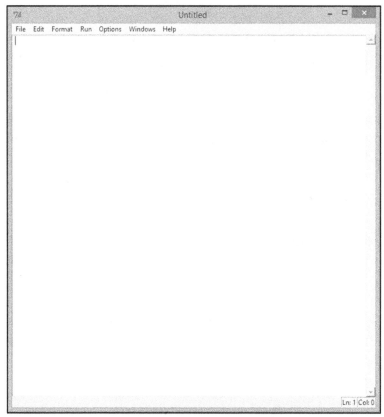

Figure 1-2: IDLE's source code editor

1.3.2.   Spyder

"Spyder" (previously known as "Pydee") stands for "Scientific PYthon Development EnviRonment" (shown in figure 1-3), and it is a powerful IDE for the Python language with advanced editing, interactive testing, debugging and introspection features. This IDE also has support of "IPython" (enhanced interactive Python interpreter) and popular Python libraries such as NumPy, Matplotlib (interactive 2D/3D plotting) etc. Some of the key features are:

- Syntax coloring (or highlighting).
- Typing helpers like automatically inserting closing parentheses etc.
- Support IPython interpreter.
- Contains basic terminal command window.

Spyder runs on all major platforms (Windows, Mac OSX, Linux), and the easiest way to install Spyder in Windows is through Python(x,y) package (visit *http://www.pythonxy.com*).

Figure 1-3: Spyder IDE

The expressions/codes discussed in this book are written and tested in Spyder IDE.

1.4. Python download and installation

There are many different ways to install Python, the best approach depends upon the operating system one is using, what is already installed, and how the person intends to use it. To avoid wading through all the details, the easiest approach is to use one of the pre-packaged Python distribution that provide built-in required libraries. An excellent choice for Windows operating system user is to install using a binary file which can be downloaded from official Python's website (*http://www.python.org/download/*).

One can install IDLE and Spyder in Ubuntu (Linux) operating system by executing the following commands in the terminal (as shown in figure 1-4).

```
sudo apt-get install idle-python2.7 spyder
```

These can be independently installed using separate commands.

```
sudo apt-get install idle-python2.7
sudo apt-get install spyder
```

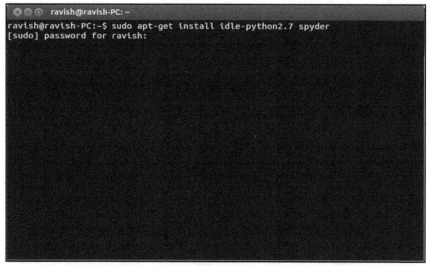

Figure 1-4: Python IDEs installation using command line terminal

1.5. Python(x,y)

"Python(x,y)" is a free scientific and engineering development software for numerical computations, data analysis and data visualization based on Python programming language and Spyder interactive development environment, the launcher (current version 2.7.6.0) is shown in figure 1-5. The executable file of Python(x,y) can be downloaded and then installed from the website link: *http://code.google.com/p/pythonxy/*. The main features of Python(x,y) are:

- Bundled with scientific oriented Python libraries and development environment tools.
- Extensive documentation of various Python packages.
- Providing all-in-one setup program, so that the user can install or uninstall all these packages and features by clicking one button only.

Figure 1-5: Python(x,y) launcher

1.6. Object

"Object" (also called "name") is Python's abstraction for data. All data in a Python program is represented by objects or by relations between objects. Every object has an identity, a type and a value. An object's identity never changes once it has been created; it can be thought of it as the object's address in memory. The `id()` function returns an integer representing its identity (currently implemented as its address). An object's type determines the operations that the object supports and also defines the possible values for objects of that type. An object's type is also unchangeable and the `type()` function returns an object's type. The value of some objects can change. Objects whose value can change are said to be "mutable"; objects whose value is unchangeable once they are created are called "immutable". In the example below, object `a` has identity `31082544`, type `int` and value 5.

```
>>> a=5
>>> id(a)
31082544
>>> type(a)
<type 'int'>
```

Some objects contain references to other objects; these are called "containers". Examples of containers are tuples, lists and dictionaries. The value of an immutable container object that contains a reference to a mutable object can change when the latter's value is changed; however the container is still considered immutable, because the collection of objects it contains cannot be changed. So, immutability is not strictly the same as having an unchangeable value.

An object has attribute(s), which are referenced using dotted expressions. For example, if an object `abc` has an attribute `pq`, then it would be referenced as `abc.pq`. In the following example, `upper()` is an attribute of `var` object.

```
>>> var='hello'
>>> var.upper()
'HELLO'
```

In the above example, `upper()` is function on some object `var`, and this function is called "method". More information on "method" is given in chapter 6.

1.7. Interactive mode

One of Python's most useful features is its interactive interpreter. It allows very fast testing of ideas without the overhead of creating test files, as is typical in most programming languages. However, the interpreter supplied with the standard Python distribution is somewhat limited for extended interactive use. IPython is a good choice for comprehensive environment for interactive and exploratory computing.

To start interactive mode, launch Python with no arguments (possibly by selecting it from your computer's main menu). It is a very powerful way to test out new ideas or inspect modules and packages.

Interactive mode prompts for the next command with the "primary prompt", usually three greater-than signs (>>>); a continuation line is prompted with the "secondary prompt", which is by default represented by three dots (. . .). The interpreter prints a welcome message stating its version number and some additional information before printing the first prompt:

```
$ python
Python 2.7 (#1, Feb 28 2010, 00:02:06)
Type   "help",   "copyright",   "credits"   or   "license"   for   more
information.
>>>
```

Continuation lines are needed when entering a multi-line statement. As an example, take a look at this `if` statement:

```
>>> the_world_is_flat = 1
>>> if the_world_is_flat:
...        print("Be careful not to fall off!")
...
Be careful not to fall off!
```

1.7.1. Invoking Python interpreter

In Unix/Linux platforms, the Python interpreter is usually installed at */usr/local/bin/python*. It is possible to start interpreter by typing the following command (same command for MS Windows)

```
$ python
```

in the shell. Since the choice of the directory where the interpreter lives is an installation option, other places are possible (e.g., */usr/local/python* is a popular alternative location).

On Windows machines, the Python installation is available at path *C:\Python27*, though, this can be changed when running the installer. To add this directory to *Path* environmental variable, type the following command into the MS DOS command prompt:

```
set path=%path%;C:\python27
```

Inputting end-of-file character (*Control-D* on Unix, *Control-Z* on Windows) at the primary prompt causes the interpreter to exit. If that does not work, you can exit the interpreter by typing the following command:

```
>>> quit()
```

1.8. Script mode

If Python interpreter is closed and then invoked again, the definitions that were made (functions, variables etc.) are lost. Therefore, to write a long program, the programmer should use a text editor to prepare the input for the interpreter and run it with that file as input instead. This is known as creating a "script". Most of the examples in this book are discussed using interactive mode, but few scripts are also incorporated.

1.8.1. First program

This section will demonstrate to write a simple Python program, which prints "Hello World". Type the following lines in IDLE text editor and save it as "HelloWorld.py".

```
#! /usr/bin/env python
print('Hello world')
```

The first line is called "shebang line" or "hashbang line" (more information in next section). The second line gives the output: "Hello World". There are numerous ways to run a Python program. The simplest approach is to press *F5* functional key after saving the program in IDLE text editor. The output is shown below:

```
>>>
Hello world
```

1.9. Executing Python script

As discussed in previous section, Python script can be executed using *F5* functional key, from Python's IDE. It can also be executed using command prompt by typing the following command:

```
$ python <filename>
```

On different platforms, the execution of Python scripts (apart from running from inside Python's IDE) can be carried out as follows:

1.9.1. Linux

On Unix/Linux system, Python script can be made directly executable, like shell scripts, by including the following expression as first line of the script (assuming that the interpreter is on the user's PATH) and giving the file an executable mode.

```
#! /usr/bin/env python
```

The '#!' must be the first two characters of the file. Note that the hash or pound character '#' is used to start a comment in Python. The script can be given an executable mode/permission, using the chmod command:

```
$ chmod +x HelloWorld.py
```

1.9.2. Windows

On Windows system, the Python installer automatically associates .py files with python.exe, so that double-click on a Python file will run it as a script. The extension can also be .pyw, in that case, the console window that normally appears is suppressed. At MS DOS prompt, the Python script can be executed by going to the directory containing the script and just entering the script name (with extension).

1.10. EBNF

A "syntactic metalanguage" is a notation for defining the syntax of a language by use of a number of rules. A syntactic metalanguage is an important tool of computer science. Since the definition of the programming language "Algol 60", it has been a custom to define the syntax of a programming language formally. Algol 60 was defined with a notation now known as "Backus-Naur Form" (BNF). This notation has proved a suitable basis for subsequent languages, but has frequently been extended or slightly altered. There are many different notations which are confusing and has prevented the advantages of formal unambiguous definitions from being widely appreciated. "Extended BNF" (abbreviated as EBNF, based on Backus-Naur Form) brings some order to the formal definition of syntax and is useful not just for the definition of programming languages, but for many other formal definitions. Please refer international standard document (ISO/IEC 14977:1996(E)) for detailed information on EBNF (website link: *http://standards.iso.org/ittf/PubliclyAvailableStandards/*).

Chapter 2
BASICS OF PYTHON

The previous chapter has given a brief introduction about Python's user interface. This chapter will scratch the surface of Python programming and expose the basic elements which a programmer needs to know beforehand.

2.1. Variable, identifier and literal

A variable is a storage location that has an associated symbolic name (called "identifier"), which contains some value (can be literal or other data) that can change. An identifier is a name used to identify a variable, function, class, module or other object. Literal is a notation for constant values of some built-in type. Literal can be string, plain integer, long integer, floating point number, imaginary number. For e.g., in the expressions

```
var1=5
var2='Tom'
```

var1 and var2 are identifiers, while 5 and 'Tom' are integer and string literals, respectively.

Consider a scenario where a variable is referenced by the identifier a and the variable contains a list. If the same variable is referenced by the identifier b as well, and if an element in the list is changed, the change will be reflected in both identifiers of same variable.

```
>>> a=[1,2,3]
>>> b=a
>>> b
[1, 2, 3]
>>> a[1]=10
>>> a
[1, 10, 3]
>>> b
[1, 10, 3]
```

Now, the above scenario can be modified a bit, where a and b are two different variables.

```
>>> a=[1,2,3]
>>> b=a[:]        # Copying data from a to b.
>>> b
[1, 2, 3]
>>> a[1]=10
>>> a
[1, 10, 3]
>>> b
[1, 2, 3]
```

There are some rules that need to be followed for valid identifier naming:
- The first character of the identifier must be a letter of the alphabet (uppercase or lowercase) or an underscore ('_').
- The rest of the identifier name can consist of letters (uppercase or lowercase character), underscores ('_') or digits (0-9).
- Identifier names are case-sensitive. For example, `myname` and `myName` are not the same.
- Identifiers can be of unlimited length.

2.2.   Token
A token is a string of one or more characters that is significant as a group. Consider an expression:

```
sum=6+2
```

The tokens in the above expression are given in table 2-1:

Table 2-1: Tokens

Token	Token type
sum	Identifier
=	Assignment operator
6	Integer literal
+	Addition operator
2	Integer literal

The process of converting a sequence of characters into a sequence of tokens is called "lexical analysis". A program or function that performs lexical analysis is called a lexical analyzer, lexer, or tokenizer. A lexer is generally combined with a parser (beyond the scope of this book), which together analyze the syntax of computer language. Python supports the following categories of tokens: NEWLINE, INDENT, DEDENT, identifiers, keywords, literals, operators, and delimiters.

2.3.   Keywords
The following identifiers (as shown as output in the following code) are used as reserved words (or "keywords") of the language, and cannot be used as ordinary identifiers.

```
>>> import keyword
>>> for kwd in keyword.kwlist:
...     print kwd
...
and
as
assert
break
class
continue
def
del
elif
else
```

```
except
exec
finally
for
from
global
if
import
in
is
lambda
not
or
pass
print
raise
return
try
while
with
yield
```

One can also check if an identifier is keyword or not using `iskeyword()` function.

```
>>> import keyword
>>> keyword.iskeyword('hi')
False
>>> keyword.iskeyword('print')
True
```

2.4. Operators and operands

An operator is a symbol (such as +, ×, etc.) that represents an operation. An operation is an action or procedure which produces a new value from one or more input values called operands. There are two types of operators: unary and binary. Unary operator operates only on one operand, such as negation. On the other hand, binary operator operates on two operands, which includes addition, subtraction, multiplication, division, exponentiation operators etc. Consider an expression 3+8, here 3 and 8 are called operands, while '+' is called operator. The operators can also be categorized into:

- Arithmetic operators.
- Comparison (or Relational) operators.
- Assignment operators.
- Logical operators.
- Bitwise operators.
- Membership operators.
- Identity operators.

2.4.1. Arithematics operators

Table 2-2 enlists the arithematic operators with a short note on the operators.

Table 2-2: Arithematic operators

Operator	Description
+	Addition operator- Add operands on either side of the operator.
-	Subtraction operator - Subtract right hand operand from left hand operand.
*	Multiplication operator - Multiply operands on either side of the operator.
/	Division operator - Divide left hand operand by right hand operand.
%	Modulus operator - Divide left hand operand by right hand operand and return remainder.
**	Exponent operator – Perform exponential (power) calculation on operands.
//	Floor Division operator - The division of operands where the result is the quotient in which the digits after the decimal point are removed.

The following example illustrates the use of the above discussed operators.

```
>>> a=20
>>> b=45.0
>>> a+b
65.0
>>> a-b
-25.0
>>> a*b
900.0
>>> b/a
2.25
>>> b%a
5.0
>>> a**b
3.5184372088832e+58
>>> b//a
2.0
```

2.4.2. Relational operators

A relational operator is an operator that tests some kind of relation between two operands. Table 2-3 enlist the relational operators with description.

Table 2-3: Relational operators

Operator	Description
==	Check if the values of two operands are equal.
!=	Check if the values of two operands are not equal.
<>	Check if the value of two operands are not equal (same as != operator).
>	Check if the value of left operand is greater than the value of right operand.
<	Check if the value of left operand is less than the value of right operand.
>=	Check if the value of left operand is greater than or equal to the value of right operand.
<=	Check if the value of left operand is less than or equal to the value of right operand.

The following example illustrates the use of the above discussed operators.

```
>>> a,b=20,40
```

```
>>> a==b
False
>>> a!=b
True
>>> a<>b
True
>>> a>b
False
>>> a<b
True
>>> a>=b
False
>>> a<=b
True
```

2.4.3. Assignment operators

Assignment operator is an operator which is used to bind or rebind names to values. Augmented assignment is the combination, in a single statement, of a binary operation and an assignment statement. An augmented assignment expression like x+=1 can be rewritten as x=x+1. Table 2-4 enlist the assignment operators with description.

Table 2-4: Assignment operators

Operator	Description
=	Assignment operator- Assigns values from right side operand to left side operand.
+=	Augmented assignment operator- It adds right side operand to the left side operand and assign the result to left side operand.
-=	Augmented assignment operator- It subtracts right side operand from the left side operand and assign the result to left side operand.
*=	Augmented assignment operator- It multiplies right side operand with the left side operand and assign the result to left side operand.
/=	Augmented assignment operator- It divides left side operand with the right side operand and assign the result to left side operand.
%=	Augmented assignment operator- It takes modulus using two operands and assign the result to left side operand.
**=	Augmented assignment operator- Performs exponential (power) calculation on operands and assigns value to the left side operand.
//=	Augmented assignment operator- Performs floor division on operators and assigns value to the left side operand.

The following example illustrates the use of the above discussed operators.

```
>>> a,b=20,40
>>> c=a+b
>>> c
60
>>> a,b=2.0,4.5
>>> c=a+b
```

```
>>> c
6.5
>>> c+=a
>>> c
8.5
>>> c-=a
>>> c
6.5
>>> c*=a
>>> c
13.0
>>> c/=a
>>> c
6.5
>>> c%=a
>>> c
0.5
>>> c**=a
>>> c
0.25
>>> c//=a
>>> c
0.0
```

2.4.4. Bitwise operators

A bitwise operator operates on one or more bit patterns or binary numerals at the level of their individual bits. Table 2-5 enlist the bitwise operators with description.

Table 2-5: Bitwise operators

Operator	Description
&	Binary AND operator- Copies corresponding binary 1 to the result, if it exists in both operands.
|	Binary OR operator- Copies corresponding binary 1 to the result, if it exists in either operand.
^	Binary XOR operator- Copies corresponding binary 1 to the result, if it is set in one operand, but not both.
~	Binary ones complement operator- It is unary and has the effect of flipping bits.
<<	Binary left shift operator- The left side operand bits are moved to the left side by the number on right side operand.
>>	Binary right shift operator- The left side operand bits are moved to the right side by the number on right side operand.

The following example illustrates the use of the above discussed operators.

```
>>> a,b=60,13
>>> a&b
12
>>> a|b
```

```
61
>>> a^b
49
>>> ~a
-61
>>> a<<2
240
>>> a>>2
15
```

In the above example, the binary representation of variables a and b are 00111100 and 00001101, respectively. The above binary operations example is tabulated in table 2-6.

Table 2-6: Bitwsie operation

Bitwise operation	Binary representation	Decimal representation
a&b	00001100	12
a|b	00111101	61
a^b	00110001	49
~a	11000011	-61
a<<2	11110000	240
a>>2	00001111	15

2.4.5. Logical operators

Logical operators compare boolean expressions and return a boolean result. Table 2-6 enlist the logical operators with description.

Table 2-7: Logical operators

Operator	Description
and	Logical AND operator- If both the operands are true (or non-zero), then condition becomes true.
or	Logical OR operator- If any of the two operands is true (or non-zero), then condition becomes true.
not	Logical NOT operator- The result is reverse of the logical state of its operand. If the operand is true (or non-zero), then condition becomes false.

The following example illustrates the use of the above discussed operators.

```
>>> 5>2 and 4<8
True
>>> 5>2 or 4>8
True
>>> not(5>2)
False
```

2.4.6. Membership operators

Membership operator is an operator which test for membership in a sequence, such as string, list, tuple etc. Table 2-7 enlists the membership operators.

Table 2-8: Membership operators

Operator	Description
in	Evaluate to true, if it find a variable in the specified sequence; otherwise false.
not in	Evaluate to true, if it does not find a variable in the specified sequence; otherwise false.

The following example illustrates the use of the above discussed operators.

```
>>> 5 in [0,5,10,15]
True
>>> 6 in [0,5,10,15]
False
>>> 5 not in [0,5,10,15]
False
>>> 6 not in [0,5,10,15]
True
```

2.4.7. Identity operators

Identity operators compare the memory locations of two objects. Table 2-8 provides a list of identity operators including a small explanation.

Table 2-9: Identity operators

Operator	Description
is	Evaluates to true, if the operands on either side of the operator point to the same object, and false otherwise.
is not	Evaluates to false, if the operands on either side of the operator point to the same object, and true otherwise.

The following example illustrates the use of the above discussed operators.

```
>>> a=b=3.1
>>> a is b
True
>>> id(a)
30984528
>>> id(b)
30984528
>>> c,d=3.1,3.1
>>> c is d
False
>>> id(c)
35058472
>>> id(d)
30984592
>>> c is not d
True
>>> a is not b
False
```

2.4.8. Operator precedence

Operator precedence determines how an expression is evaluated. Certain operators have higher precedence than others; for example, the multiplication operator has higher precedence than the addition operator. In the expression x=7+3*2, x is assigned 13, not 20, because operator * has higher precedence than +, so it first multiplies 3*2 and then adds into 7.

Table 2-10 summarizes the operator's precedence in Python, from lowest precedence to highest precedence (from top to bottom). Operators in the same box have the same precedence.

Table 2-10: Operator precedence

Operator
not, or, and
in, not in
is, is not
=, %, =/, =//, -=, +=, *=, **=
<>, ==, !=
<=, <, >, >=
^,	
&
>>, <<
+, -
*, /, %, //
~, +, -
**

2.5. Delimiters

Delimiter is a character that separates and organizes items of data. An example of a delimiter is the comma character, which acts as a field delimiter in a sequence of comma-separated values. Table 2-11 provides a list of tokens which serves as delimiters in Python.

Table 2-11: Delimiters

Delimiters													
(	)	[	]	@	{	}	,	:	.	`	;	=	
+=	-=	*=	/=	//=	%=	&=	|=	^=	>>=	<<=	**=		

The following example shows how the use of delimeters can affect the result.

```
>>> 5+6/2            # no delimiter used
8.0
>>> (5+6)/2          # delimiter used
5.5
```

Following are few points that a Python programmer should be aware of:
-   The period (.) can also occur in floating-point and imaginary literals.

- The simple and augmented assignment operators, serve lexically as delimiters, but also perform operations.
- ASCII characters ', ", #, and \ have special meaning as part of other tokens or are otherwise significant to the lexical analyzer.
- Whitespace is not a token, but serve to delimit tokens.

2.6. Line structure

A Python program is divided into a number of logical lines.

2.6.1. Physical and logical lines

A physical line is a sequence of characters terminated by an end-of-line sequence. The end of a logical line is represented by the token NEWLINE. A logical line is ignored (i.e. no NEWLINE token is generated) that contains only spaces, tabs, or a comment. This is called "blank line". The following code

```
>>> i=5
>>> print(5)
5
```

is same as:

```
>>> i=5; print(i)
5
```

A logical line is constructed from one or more physical lines by following the explicit or implicit line joining rules.

2.6.1.1. Explicit line joining

Two or more physical lines may be joined into logical lines using backslash characters (\), as shown in the following example:

```
>>> if 1900 < year < 2100 and 1 <= month <= 12 \
... and 1 <= day <= 31 and 0 <= hour < 24 \
... and 0 <= minute < 60 and 0 <= second < 60:
...         print year
```

A line ending in a backslash cannot carry a comment. Also, backslash does not continue a comment. A backslash does not continue a token except for string literals (i.e., tokens other than string literals cannot be split across physical lines using a backslash). A backslash is illegal elsewhere on a line outside a string literal.

```
>>> str='This is a \
... string example'
>>> str
'This is a string example'
```

2.6.1.2. Implicit line joining

Expressions in parentheses, square brackets or curly braces can be split over more than one physical line without using backslashes. For example:

```
>>> month_names=['Januari','Februari','Maart',      # These are the
...              'April','Mei','Juni',               # Dutch names
...              'Juli','Augustus','September',       # for the months
...              'Oktober','November','December']     # of the year
```

Implicitly continued lines can carry comments. The indentation of the continuation lines is not important. Blank continuation lines are allowed. There is no NEWLINE token between implicit continuation lines. Implicitly continued lines can also occur within triple-quoted strings; in that case they cannot carry comments.

```
>>> str="""This is
... a string
... example"""
>>> str
'This is \na string \nexample'
>>> str='''This is
... a string
... example'''
>>> str
'This is \na string \nexample'
```

2.6.2. Comment

A comment starts with a hash character (#) that is not part of a string literal, and terminates at the end of the physical line. A comment signifies the end of the logical line unless the implicit line joining rules are invoked. Also, comments are not executed.

2.6.3. Indentation

Whitespace is important in Python. Actually, whitespace at the beginning of the line is important. This is called indentation. Leading whitespace (spaces and tabs) at the beginning of the logical line is used to determine the indentation level of the logical line, which in turn is used to determine the grouping of statements. This means that statements which go together must have the same indentation. Each such set of statements is a block. One thing should be remembered is that wrong indentation can give rise to error (IndentationError exception).

```
>>> i=10
>>> print "Value is ",i
Value is  10
>>>  print "Value is ",i
  File "<stdin>", line 1
    print "Value is ",i
    ^
IndentationError: unexpected indent
```

The indentation levels of consecutive lines are used to generate INDENT and DEDENT tokens. One can observe that by inserting whitespace in the beginning gave rise to `IndentationError` exception.

The following example shows non-uniform indentation is not an error.

```
>>> var=100
>>> if var!=100:
...     print 'var does not have value 100'
... else:
...                 print 'var has value 100'
...
var has value 100
```

2.6.3.1. Need for indentation

In *C* programming language, there are numerous ways to place the braces for grouping of statements. If a programmer is habitual of reading and writing code that uses one style, he or she will feel at least slightly uneasy when reading (or being required to write) another style. Many coding styles place begin/end brackets on a line by themselves. This makes programs considerably longer and wastes valuable screen space, making it harder to get a good overview of a program.

Guido van Rossum believes that using indentation for grouping is extremely elegant and contributes a lot to the clarity of the typical Python program. Since there are no begin/end brackets, there cannot be a disagreement between grouping perceived by the parser and the human reader. Also, Python is much less prone to coding-style conflicts.

2.7. Built-in types

This section describes the standard data types that are built into the interpreter. There are various built-in data types, for e.g., numeric, sequence, mapping, etc., but this book will cover few types. Schematic representation of various built-in types is shown in figure 2-1.

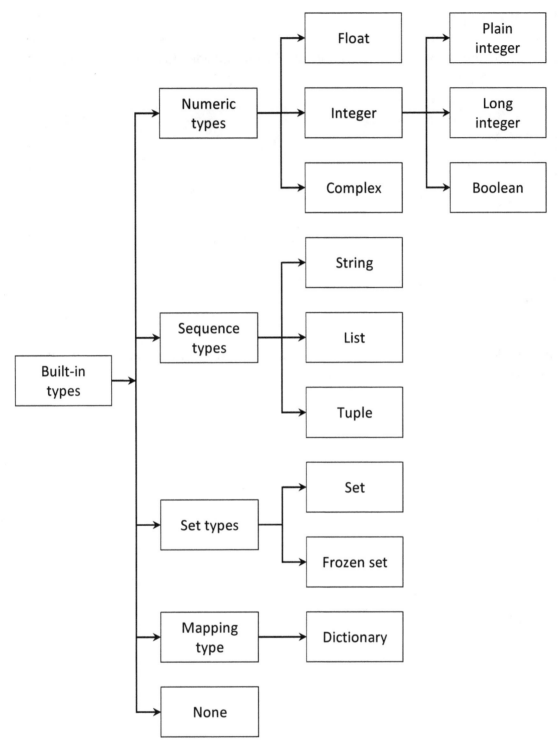

Figure 2-1: Schematic representation of built-in types

2.7.1. Numeric types

There are three distinct numeric types: integer, floating point number, and complex number.

2.7.1.1. Integer

Integer can be sub-classified into three types:

2.7.1.1.1. Plain integer

Plain integer (or simply "integer") represents integer number in the range -2147483648 through 2147483647. When the result of an operation would fall outside this range, the result is normally returned as a long integer.

```
>>> a=2147483647
>>> type(a)
<type 'int'>
>>> a=a+1
>>> type(a)
<type 'long'>
>>> a=-2147483648
>>> type(a)
<type 'int'>
>>> a=a-1
>>> type(a)
<type 'long'>
```

The built-in function `int(x=0)` convert a number or string `x` to an integer, or return 0, if no arguments are given.

```
>>> a='57'
>>> type(a)
<type 'str'>
>>> a=int(a)
>>> a
57
>>> type(a)
<type 'int'>
>>> a=5.7
>>> type(a)
<type 'float'>
>>> a=int(a)
>>> a
5
>>> type(a)
<type 'int'>
>>> int()
0
```

2.7.1.1.2. Long integer

This represents integer numbers in virtually unlimited range, subject to available memory. The built-in function `long(x=0)` convert a string or number to a long integer. If the argument is a string, it must contain a possibly signed number. If no argument is given, `0L` is returned.

```
>>> a=5
>>> type(a)
<type 'int'>
```

```
>>> a=long(a)
>>> a
5L
>>> type(a)
<type 'long'>
>>> long()
0L
>>> long(5)
5L
>>> long(5.8)
5L
>>> long('5')
5L
>>> long('-5')
-5L
```

Integer literals with an L or l suffix yield long integers (L is preferred because 1l looks too much like eleven).

```
>>> a=10L
>>> type(a)
<type 'long'>
>>> a=10l
>>> type(a)
<type 'long'>
```

The following expressions are interesting.

```
>>> import sys
>>> a=sys.maxint
>>> a
2147483647
>>> type(a)
<type 'int'>
>>> a=a+1
>>> a
2147483648L
>>> type(a)
<type 'long'>
```

2.7.1.1.3. Boolean

This represents the truth values False and True. The boolean type is a sub-type of plain integer, and boolean values behave like the values 0 and 1. The built-in function bool() convert a value to boolean, using the standard truth testing procedure.

```
>>> bool()
False
>>> a=5
```

```
>>> bool(a)
True
>>> bool(0)
False
>>> bool('hi')
True
>>> bool(None)
False
>>> bool('')
False
>>> bool(False)
False
>>> bool("False")
True
>>> bool(5>3)
True
```

2.7.1.2. Floating point number

This represents decimal point number. Python supports only double-precision floating point number (occupies 8 bytes of memory) and does not support single-precision floating point number (occupies 4 bytes of memory). The built-in function `float()` convert a string or a number to floating point number.

```
>>> a=57
>>> type(a)
<type 'int'>
>>> a=float(a)
>>> a
57.0
>>> type(a)
<type 'float'>
>>> a='65'
>>> type(a)
<type 'str'>
>>> a=float(a)
>>> a
65.0
>>> type(a)
<type 'float'>
>>> a=1e308
>>> a
1e+308
>>> type(a)
<type 'float'>
>>> a=1e309
>>> a
inf
>>> type(a)
<type 'float'>
```

2.7.1.3. Complex number

This represents complex numbers having real and imaginary parts. The built-in function `complex()` is used to convert number or string to complex number.

```
>>> a=5.3
>>> a=complex(a)
>>> a
(5.3+0j)
>>> type(a)
<type 'complex'>
>>> a=complex()
>>> a
0j
>>> type(a)
<type 'complex'>
```

Appending j or J to a numeric literal yields a complex number.

```
>>> a=3.4j
>>> a
3.4j
>>> type(a)
<type 'complex'>
>>> a=3.5+4.9j
>>> type(a)
<type 'complex'>
>>> a=3.5+4.9J
>>> type(a)
<type 'complex'>
```

The real and imaginary parts of a complex number z can be retrieved through the attributes `z.real` and `z.imag`.

```
a=3.5+4.9J
>>> a.real
3.5
>>> a.imag
4.9
```

2.7.2. Sequence Types

These represent finite ordered sets, usually indexed by non-negative numbers. When the length of a sequence is n, the index set contain the numbers 0, 1, ..., n-1. Item i of sequence a is selected by `a[i]`. There are seven sequence types: string, Unicode string, list, tuple, bytearray, buffer, and xrange objects.

Sequence can be mutable or immutable. Immutable sequence is a sequence that cannot be changed after it is created. If immutable sequence object contains references to other objects, these other objects may be mutable and may be changed; however, the collection of objects directly referenced by an immutable object cannot change. Mutable sequence is a sequence that can be changed after it is created. There are two intrinsic mutable sequence types: list and byte array.

Iterable is an object capable of returning its members one at a time. Examples of iterables include all sequence types (such as `list`, `str`, and `tuple`) and some non-sequence types like `dict` and `file` etc. Iterables can be used in a `for` loop and in many other places where a sequence is needed (`zip()`, `map()`, ...). When an iterable object is passed as an argument to the built-in function `iter()`, it returns an iterator for the object. An iterator is an object representing a stream of data; repeated calls to the iterator's `next()` method return successive items in the stream. When no more data are available, `StopIteration` exception is raised instead.

Some of the sequence types are discussed below:

2.7.2.1. String
It is a sequence type such that its value can be characters, symbols, or numbers. Please note that string is immutable.

```
>>> a='Python : 2.7'
>>> type(a)
<type 'str'>
>>> a[2]='S'
Traceback (most recent call last):
  File "<stdin>", line 1, in <module>
TypeError: 'str' object does not support item assignment
```

The built-in function `str(object='')` return a string containing a nicely printable representation of an `object`. For strings, this returns the string itself. If no argument is given, an empty string is returned.

```
>>> a=57.3
>>> type(a)
<type 'float'>
>>> a=str(a)
>>> a
'57.3'
>>> type(a)
<type 'str'>
```

2.7.2.2. Tuple
Tuple is comma-separated sequence of arbitrary Python objects enclosed in parenthesis (round brackets). Please note that tuple is immutable. Tuple is discussed in detail in chapter 4.

```
>>> a=(1,2,3,4)
>>> type(a)
<type 'tuple'>
'a', 'b', 'c')
```

2.7.2.3. List

List is comma-separated sequence of arbitrary Python objects enclosed in square brackets. Please note that list is mutable. More information on list is provided in chapter 4.

```
>>> a=[1,2,3,4]
>>> type(a)
<type 'list'>
```

2.7.3. Set types

These represent unordered, finite set of unique objects. As such, it cannot be indexed by any subscript, however they can be iterated over. Common uses of set are fast membership testing, removing duplicates from a sequence, and computing mathematical operations such as intersection, union, difference, and symmetric difference. There are two set types:

2.7.3.1. Set

This represents a mutable set. It is created by the built-in function `set()`, and can be modified afterward by several methods, such as `add()`, `remove()` etc. More information on set is given in chapter 4.

```
>>> set1=set()                      # A new empty set
>>> set1.add("cat")                 # Add a single member
>>> set1.update(["dog","mouse"])    # Add several members
>>> set1.remove("mouse")            # Remove member
>>> set1
set(['dog', 'cat'])
>>> set2=set(["dog","mouse"])
>>> print set1&set2                 # Intersection
set(['dog'])
>>> print set1|set2                 # Union
set(['mouse', 'dog', 'cat'])
```

The `set([iterable])` return a new `set` object, optionally with elements taken from `iterable`.

2.7.3.2. Frozenset

This represents an immutable set. It is created by built-in function `frozenset()`. As a frozenset is immutable, it can be used again as an element of another set, or as dictionary key.

```
>>> frozenset()
frozenset([])
>>> frozenset('aeiou')
frozenset(['a', 'i', 'e', 'u', 'o'])
>>> frozenset([0, 0, 0, 44, 0, 44, 18])
frozenset([0, 18, 44])
```

The `frozenset([iterable])` return return a new `frozenset` object, optionally with elements taken from `iterable`.

2.7.4. Mapping Types

This represents a container object that support arbitrary key lookups. The notation `a[k]` select the value indexed by key `k` from the mapping `a`; this can be used in expressions and as the target of assignments or `del` statements. The built-in function `len()` returns the number of items in a mapping. Currently, there is a single mapping type:

2.7.4.1. Dictionary

A dictionary is a mutable collection of unordered values accessed by key rather than by index. In dictionary, arbitrary keys are mapped to values. More information is provided in chapter 4.

```
>>> dict1={"john":34,"mike":56}
>>> dict1["michael"]=42
>>> dict1
{'mike': 56, 'john': 34, 'michael': 42}
>>> dict1["mike"]
56
```

2.7.5. None

This signifies the absence of a value in a situation, e.g., it is returned from a function that does not explicitly return anything. Its truth value is `False`.

Some other built-in types such as function, method, class, class instance, file, module etc. are discussed in later chapters.

2.8. Integer function

The following function operates on integer (plain and long).

`int.bit_length()`
Return the number of bits necessary to represent an integer (plain or long) in binary, excluding the sign and leading zeros.

```
>>> n=-37
>>> bin(n)        # bin() convert integer number to a binary string
'-0b100101'
>>> n.bit_length()
6
>>> n=2**31
>>> n
2147483648L
>>> bin(n)
'0b10000000000000000000000000000000'
>>> n.bit_length()
32
```

2.9. Float functions

Some of the functions for floating point number are discussed below.

```
float.as_integer_ratio()
```
Return a pair of integers whose ratio is exactly equal to the original float and with a positive denominator.

```
>>> (-0.25).as_integer_ratio()
(-1, 4)
```

```
float.is_integer()
```
Return `True` if the float instance is finite with integral value, otherwise it return `False`.

```
>>> (-2.0).is_integer()
True
>>> (3.2).is_integer()
False
```

2.10. String

Python can manipulate string, which can be expressed in several ways. String literals can be enclosed in matching single quotes (') or double quotes ("); e.g. `'hello'`, `"hello"` etc. They can also be enclosed in matching groups of three single or double quotes (these are generally referred to as triple-quoted strings), e.g. `'''hello'''`, `"""hello"""`. A string is enclosed in double quotes if the string contains a single quote (and no double quotes), else it is enclosed in single quotes.

```
>>> "doesnt"
'doesnt'
>>> "doesn't"
"doesn't"
>>> '"Yes," he said.'
'"Yes," he said.'
```

The above statements can also be written in some other interesting way using escape sequences.

```
>>> "doesn\'t"
"doesn't"
>>> '\"Yes,\" he said.'
'"Yes," he said.'
```

Escape sequences are character combinations that comprises of a backslash (\) followed by some character, that has special meaning, such as newline, backslash itself, or the quote character. They are called escape sequences because the backslash causes an escape from the normal way characters are interpreted by the compiler/interpreter. The `print` statement produces a more readable output for such input strings. Table 2-12 mentions some of the escape sequences.

Table 2-12: Escape sequence

Escape sequence	Meaning
\n	Newline.
\t	Horizontal tab.

Escape sequence	Meaning
\v	Vertical tab.
\\	Backslash (\).
\'	Single quote (').
\"	Double quote (").

String literal may optionally be prefixed with a letter r or R , such string is called raw string, and there is no escaping of character by backslash.

```
>>> str='This is \n a string'
>>> print str
This is
 a string
>>> str=r'This is \n a string'
>>> print str
This is \n a string
```

Specifically, a raw string cannot end in a single backslash.

```
>>> str=r'\'
  File "<stdin>", line 1
    str=r'\'
           ^
SyntaxError: EOL while scanning string literal
```

Triple quotes are used to specify multi-line string. One can use single quotes and double quotes freely within the triple quotes.

```
>>> line="""This is
... a triple
... quotes example"""
>>> line
'This is\na triple\nquotes example'
>>> print line
This is
a triple
quotes example
```

Unicode strings are not discussed in this book, but just for the information that a prefix of 'u' or 'U' makes the string a Unicode string.

The string module contains a number of useful constants and functions for string based operations. Also, for string functions based on regular expressions, refer re module. Both string and re modules are discussed later in this chapter.

2.10.1. String operations
Some of the string operations supported by Python are discussed below.

2.10.1.1. Concatenation
Strings can be concatenated using + operator.

```
>>> word='Python'+' Program'
>>> word
'Python Program'
```

Two string literals next to each other are automatically concatenated; this only works with two literals, not with arbitrary string expressions.

```
>>> 'Python' ' Program'
'Python Program'
>>> word1='Python'
>>> word2='Program'
>>> word1 word2
  File "<stdin>", line 1
    word1 word2
             ^
SyntaxError: invalid syntax
```

2.10.1.2. Repetition
Strings can be repeated with * operator.

```
>>> word='Help '
>>> word*3
'Help Help Help '
>>> 3*word
'Help Help Help '
```

2.10.1.3. Membership operation
As discussed previously, membership operators in and not in are used to test for membership in a sequence.

```
>>> word='Python'
>>> 'th' in word
True
>>> 'T' not in word
True
```

2.10.1.4. Slicing operation
String can be indexed, the first character of a string has sub-script (index) as 0. There is no separate character type; a character is simply a string of size one. A sub-string can be specified with the slice notation.

```
>>> word='Python'
>>> word[2]
```

```
't'
>>> word[0:2]
'Py'
```

String slicing can be in form of steps, the operation `s[i:j:k]` slices the string `s` from `i` to `j` with step `k`.

```
>>> word[1:6:2]
'yhn'
```

Slice indices have useful defaults, an omitted first index defaults to zero, an omitted second index defaults to the size of the string being sliced.

```
>>> word[:2]
'Py'
>>> word[2:]
'thon'
```

As mentioned earlier, string is immutable, however, creating a new string with the combined content is easy and efficient.

```
>>> word[0]='J'
Traceback (most recent call last):
  File "<stdin>", line 1, in <module>
TypeError: 'str' object does not support item assignment
>>> 'J'+word[1:]
'Jython'
```

If upper bound is greater than length of string, then it is replaced by the string size; an upper bound smaller than the lower bound returns an empty string.

```
>>> word[2:50]
'thon'
>>> word[4:1]
''
```

Indices can be negative numbers, which indicates counting from the right hand side.

```
>>> word[-1]
'n'
>>> word[-2]
'o'
>>> word[-3:]
'hon'
>>> word[:-3]
'Pyt'
>>> word[-0]    # -0 is same as 0
'P'
```

Out of range negative slice indices are truncated, but single element (non-slice) index raises `IndexError` exception.

```
>>> word[-100:]
'Python'
>>> word[-100]
Traceback (most recent call last):
  File "<stdin>", line 1, in <module>
IndexError: string index out of range
```

2.10.1.5. String formatting

String objects has an interesting built-in operator called modulo operator (%). This is also known as the "string formatting" or "interpolation operator". Given `format%values` (where `format` is a string object), the % conversion specifications in `format` are replaced with zero or more elements of `values`. The `%` character marks the start of the conversion specifier. If `format` requires a single argument, `values` may be a single non-tuple object. Otherwise, `values` must be a tuple with exactly the number of items specified by the `format` string, or a single mapping object (a dictionary). If dictionary is provided, then the mapping key is provided in parenthesis.

```
>>> '%s Python is a programming language.' % 'Python'
'Python Python is a programming language.'
>>> '%s Python is a programming language.' % ('Python')
'Python Python is a programming language.'
>>>
>>> '%s has %d quote types.' % ('Python',2)
'Python has 2 quote types.'
>>> '%s has %03d quote types.' % ('Python',2)
'Python has 002 quote types.'
>>> '%(language)s has %(number)03d quote types.' % \
... {"language":"Python","number":2}
'Python has 002 quote types.'
```

In the above example, 03 consists of two components:
- 0 is a conversion flag i.e. the conversion will be zero padded for numeric values.
- 3 is minimum field width (optional).

Table 2-13 shows some of the conversion types.

Table 2-13: Conversion types

Conversion	Meaning
d	Signed integer decimal.
i	Signed integer decimal.
e	Floating point exponential format (lowercase).
E	Floating point exponential format (uppercase).
f	Floating point decimal format.
F	Floating point decimal format.

Conversion	Meaning
g	Floating point format. Uses lowercase exponential format if exponent is less than -4 or not less than precision, decimal format otherwise.
G	Floating point format. Uses uppercase exponential format if exponent is less than -4 or not less than precision, decimal format otherwise.
s	String.

Precision (optional) is given as a dot (.) followed by the precision number. While using conversion type f, F, e, or E, the precision determines the number of digits after the decimal point, and it defaults to 6.

```
>>> "Today's stock price: %f" % 50
"Today's stock price: 50.000000"
>>> "Today's stock price: %F" % 50
"Today's stock price: 50.000000"
>>>
>>> "Today's stock price: %f" % 50.4625
"Today's stock price: 50.462500"
>>> "Today's stock price: %F" % 50.4625
"Today's stock price: 50.462500"
>>>
>>> "Today's stock price: %f" % 50.46251987624312359
"Today's stock price: 50.462520"
>>> "Today's stock price: %F" % 50.46251987624312359
"Today's stock price: 50.462520"
>>>
>>> "Today's stock price: %.2f" % 50.4625
"Today's stock price: 50.46"
>>> "Today's stock price: %.2F" % 50.4625
"Today's stock price: 50.46"
>>>
>>> "Today's stock price: %e" % 50.46251987624312359
"Today's stock price: 5.046252e+01"
>>> "Today's stock price: %E" % 50.46251987624312359
"Today's stock price: 5.046252E+01"
>>> "Today's stock price: %.3e" % 50.46251987624312359
"Today's stock price: 5.046e+01"
>>> "Today's stock price: %.3E" % 50.46251987624312359
"Today's stock price: 5.046E+01"
```

While using conversion type g or G, the precision determines the number of significant digits before and after the decimal point, and it defaults to 6.

```
>>> "Today's stock price: %g" % 50.46251987624312359
"Today's stock price: 50.4625"
>>> "Today's stock price: %G" % 50.46251987624312359
"Today's stock price: 50.4625"
>>>
>>> "Today's stock price: %g" % 0.000000504625198762431235
```

```
"Today's stock price: 5.04625e-07"
>>> "Today's stock price: %G" % 0.00000050462519876243l2359
"Today's stock price: 5.04625E-07"
```

2.10.2. String constants
Some constants defined in `string` module are as follows:

`string.ascii_lowercase`
It returns string containing lowercase letters `'abcdefghijklmnopqrstuvwxyz'`.

```
>>> import string
>>> string.ascii_lowercase
'abcdefghijklmnopqrstuvwxyz'
```

`string.ascii_uppercase`
It return string containing uppercase letters `'ABCDEFGHIJKLMNOPQRSTUVWXYZ'`.

```
>>> string.ascii_uppercase
'ABCDEFGHIJKLMNOPQRSTUVWXYZ'
```

`string.ascii_letters`
It returns string containing concatenation of the `ascii_lowercase` and `ascii_uppercase` constants.

```
>>> string.ascii_letters
'abcdefghijklmnopqrstuvwxyzABCDEFGHIJKLMNOPQRSTUVWXYZ'
```

`string.digits`
It returns the string containing digits `'0123456789'`.

```
>>> string.digits
'0123456789'
```

`string.hexdigits`
It returns the string containing hexadecimal characters `'0123456789abcdefABCDEF'`.

```
>>> string.hexdigits
'0123456789abcdefABCDEF'
```

`string.octdigits`
It returns the string containing octal characters `'01234567'`.

```
>>> string.octdigits
'01234567'
```

`string.punctuation`
It returns the string of ASCII characters which are considered punctuation characters.

```
>>> string.punctuation
'!"#$%&\'()*+,-./:;<=>?@[\\]^_`{|}~'
```

string.whitespace
It returns the string containing all characters that are considered whitespace like space, tab, vertical tab etc.

```
>>> string.whitespace
'\t\n\x0b\x0c\r '
```

string.printable
It returns the string of characters which are considered printable. This is a combination of digits, letters, punctuation, and whitespace.

```
>>> string.printable
'0123456789abcdefghijklmnopqrstuvwxyzABCDEFGHIJKLMNOPQRSTUVWXYZ!"#$%&
\'()*+,-./:;<=>?@[\\]^_`{|}~ \t\n\r\x0b\x0c'
```

2.10.3. String methods
Below are listed some of the string methods which supports both strings and Unicode objects. Alternatively, some of these string operations can also be accomplished using functions of `string` module.

str.isalnum()
Return `True`, if all characters in the string are alphanumeric, otherwise `False` is returned.

```
>>> str="this2009"
>>> str.isalnum()
True
>>> str="this is string example....wow!!!"
>>> str.isalnum()
False
```

str.isalpha()
Return `True`, if all characters in the string are alphabetic, otherwise `False` is returned.

```
>>> str="this"
>>> str.isalpha()
True
>>> str="this is string example....wow!!!"
>>> str.isalpha()
False
```

str.isdigit()
Return `True`, if all characters in the string are digits, otherwise `False` is returned.

```
>>> str="this2009"
```

```
>>> str.isdigit()
False
>>> str="2009"
>>> str.isdigit()
True
```

`str.isspace()`

Return `True`, if there are only whitespace characters in the string, otherwise `False` is returned.

```
>>> str="         "
>>> str.isspace()
True
>>> str="This is string example....wow!!!"
>>> str.isspace()
False
```

`str.islower()`

Return `True`, if all cased characters in the string are in lowercase and there is at least one cased character, `False` otherwise.

```
>>> str="THIS is string example....wow!!!"
>>> str.islower()
False
>>> str="this is string example....wow!!!"
>>> str.islower()
True
>>> str="this2009"
>>> str.islower()
True
>>> str="2009"
>>> str.islower()
False
```

`str.lower()`

Return a string with all the cased characters converted to lowercase.

```
>>> str="THIS IS STRING EXAMPLE....WOW!!!"
>>> str.lower()
'this is string example....wow!!!'
```

The above can be imitated using `string` module's function `string.lower(s)`, where `s` is a string.

```
>>> import string
>>> str="THIS IS STRING EXAMPLE....WOW!!!"
>>> string.lower(str)
'this is string example....wow!!!'
```

```
str.isupper()
```
Return `True`, if all cased characters in the string are uppercase and there is at least one cased character, otherwise `False` is returned.

```
>>> str="THIS IS STRING EXAMPLE....WOW!!!"
>>> str.isupper()
True
>>> str="THIS is string example....wow!!!"
>>> str.isupper()
False
```

```
str.upper()
```
Return a string with all the cased characters converted to uppercase. Note that `str.upper().isupper()` might be `False`, if string contains uncased characters.

```
>>> str="this is string example....wow!!!"
>>> str.upper()
'THIS IS STRING EXAMPLE....WOW!!!'
>>> str.upper().isupper()
True
>>> str="@1234@"
>>> str.upper()
'@1234@'
>>> str.upper().isupper()
False
```

The above can be imitated using `string` module's function `string.upper(s)`, where `s` is a string.

```
>>> str="this is string example....wow!!!"
>>> string.upper(str)
'THIS IS STRING EXAMPLE....WOW!!!'
>>> string.upper(str).isupper()
True
>>> str="@1234@"
>>> string.upper(str)
'@1234@'
>>> string.upper(str).isupper()
False
```

```
str.capitalize()
```
Return a string with its first character capitalized and the rest lower cased.

```
>>> str="this Is stRing example....wow!!!"
>>> str.capitalize()
'This is string example....wow!!!'
```

The above can be imitated using `string` module's function `string.capitalize(word)`, where `word` is a string.

```
>>> str="this Is stRing example....wow!!!"
>>> string.capitalize(str)
'This is string example....wow!!!'
```

`str.istitle()`
Return `True`, if the string is title cased, otherwise `False` is returned.

```
>>> str="This Is String Example...Wow!!!"
>>> str.istitle()
True
>>> str="This is string example....wow!!!"
>>> str.istitle()
False
```

`str.title()`
Return a title cased version of the string, where words start with an uppercase character and the remaining characters are lowercase. It will return unexpected result in cases where words have apostrophe etc.

```
>>> str="this is string example....wow!!!"
>>> str.title()
'This Is String Example....Wow!!!'
>>> str="this isn't a float example....wow!!!"
>>> str.title()
"This Isn'T A Float Example....Wow!!!"
```

`str.swapcase()`
Return a copy of the string with reversed character case.

```
>>> str="This is string example....WOW!!!"
>>> str.swapcase()
'tHIS IS STRING EXAMPLE....wow!!!'
```

The above can be imitated using `string` module's function `string.swapcase(s)`, where s is a string.

```
>>> str="This is string example....WOW!!!"
>>> string.swapcase(str)
'tHIS IS STRING EXAMPLE....wow!!!'
```

`str.count(sub[, start[, end]])`
Return the number of non-overlapping occurrences of sub-string `sub` in the range `[start, end]`. Optional arguments `start` and `end` are interpreted as in slice notation.

```
>>> str="this is string example....wow!!!"
```

```
>>> sub="i"
>>> str.count(sub,4,40)
2
>>> sub="wow"
>>> str.count(sub)
1
```

The above can be imitated using `string` module's function `string.count(s,sub[,start [,end]])`, where `s` is a string.

```
>>> str="this is string example....wow!!!"
>>> sub="i"
>>> string.count(str,sub,4,40)
2
>>> sub="wow"
>>> string.count(str,sub)
1
```

`str.find(sub[,start[,end]])`
Return the lowest index in the string where sub-string `sub` is found, such that `sub` is contained in the slice `s[start:end]`. Optional arguments `start` and `end` are interpreted as in slice notation. Return -1, if `sub` is not found.

```
>>> str1="this is string example....wow!!!"
>>> str2="exam"
>>> str1.find(str2)
15
>>> str1.find(str2,10)
15
>>> str1.find(str2,40)
-1
```

The above can be imitated using `string` module's function `string.find(s,sub[,start [,end]])`, where `s` is a string.

```
>>> str1="this is string example....wow!!!"
>>> str2="exam"
>>> string.find(str1,str2)
15
>>> string.find(str1,str2,10)
15
>>> string.find(str1,str2,40)
-1
```

The `find()` method should be used only if there is a requirement to know the position of `sub`. To check if `sub` is a sub-string or not, use the `in` operator:

```
>>> 'Py' in 'Python'
```

```
True
```

```
str.rfind(sub[,start[,end]])
```
Return the highest index in the string where sub-string `sub` is found, such that `sub` is contained within `s[start:end]`. Optional arguments `start` and `end` are interpreted as in slice notation. Return -1 on failure.

```
>>> str1="this is really a string example....wow!!!"
>>> str2="is"
>>> str1.rfind(str2)
5
>>> str1.rfind(str2,0,10)
5
>>> str1.rfind(str2,10,20)
-1
```

The above can be imitated using `string` module's function `string.rfind(s,sub[,start[,end]])`, where `s` is a string.

```
>>> str1="this is really a string example....wow!!!"
>>> str2="is"
>>> string.rfind(str1,str2)
5
>>> string.rfind(str1,str2,0,10)
5
>>> string.rfind(str1,str2,10,0)
-1
```

```
str.index(sub[,start[,end]])
```
Like `find()`, but raise `ValueError` when the sub-string is not found.

```
>>> str1="this is string example....wow!!!"
>>> str2="exam"
>>> str1.index(str2)
15
>>> str1.index(str2,10)
15
>>> str1.index(str2,40)

Traceback (most recent call last):
  File "<pyshell#38>", line 1, in <module>
    str1.index(str2, 40)
ValueError: substring not found
```

The above can be imitated using `string` module's function `string.index(s,sub[,start[,end]])`, where `s` is a string.

```
>>> str1="this is string example....wow!!!"
```

```
>>> str2="exam"
>>> string.index(str1,str2)
15
>>> string.index(str1,str2,10)
15
>>> string.index(str1,str2,40)
Traceback (most recent call last):
  File "<stdin>", line 1, in <module>
  File "C:\Python27\lib\string.py", line 328, in index
    return s.index(*args)
ValueError: substring not found
```

`str.rindex(sub[,start[,end]])`
Like `rfind()`, but raises `ValueError` when the sub-string `sub` is not found.

```
>>> str1="this is string example....wow!!!"
>>> str2="is"
>>> str1.rindex(str2)
5
>>> str1.rindex(str2,10,20)
Traceback (most recent call last):
  File "<stdin>", line 1, in <module>
ValueError: substring not found
```

The above can be imitated using `string` module's function `string.rfind(s,sub[,start[,end]])`, where s is a string.

```
>>> str1="this is string example....wow!!!"
>>> str2="is"
>>> string.rindex(str1,str2)
5
>>> string.rindex(str1,str2,10,20)
Traceback (most recent call last):
  File "<stdin>", line 1, in <module>
  File "C:\Python27\lib\string.py", line 337, in rindex
    return s.rindex(*args)
ValueError: substring not found
```

`str.startswith(prefix[,start[,end]])`
Return `True`, if string start with the `prefix`, otherwise return `False`. The `prefix` can also be a tuple of prefixes to look for. With optional `start`, test string beginning at that position. With optional `end`, stop comparing string at that position.

```
>>> str="this is string example....wow!!!"
>>> str.startswith('this')
True
>>> str.startswith('is',2)
True
>>> str.startswith('this',10,17)
```

```
False
>>> pfx=('the','where','thi')
>>> str.startswith(pfx)
True
```

`str.endswith(suffix[,start[,end]])`
Return `True`, if the string ends with the specified `suffix`, otherwise return `False`. The `suffix` can also be a tuple of suffixes to look for. The test starts from the index mentioned by optional argument `start`. The comparison is stopped indicated by optional argument `end`.

```
>>> str="this is string example....wow!!!"
>>> suffix="wow!!!"
>>> str.endswith(suffix)
True
>>> suffix=("tot!!!","wow!!!")
>>> str.endswith(suffix)
True
>>> str.endswith(suffix,20)
True
>>> suffix="is"
>>> str.endswith(suffix,2,4)
True
>>> str.endswith(suffix,2,6)
False
>>> str.endswith(('hey','bye','w!!!'))
True
```

`str.join(iterable)`
Return a string which is the concatenation of the strings in the iterable `iterable`. The separator between elements is the string `str` providing this method.

```
>>> str="-"
>>> seq=("a","b","c")
>>> str.join(seq)
'a-b-c'
>>> seq=["a","b","c"]
>>> str.join(seq)
'a-b-c'
```

The above can be imitated using `string` module's function `string.join(words[,sep])`, where `words` is a list or tuple of strings, while default value for `sep` is a single space character.

```
>>> str="-"
>>> seq=("a","b","c")
>>> string.join(seq,str)
'a-b-c'
>>> seq=["a","b","c"]
>>> string.join(seq,str)
'a-b-c'
```

`str.replace(old,new[,count])`
Return a string with all occurrences of sub-string `old` replaced by `new`. If the optional argument `count` is given, only the first `count` occurrences are replaced.

```
>>> str="this is string example....wow!!! this is really string"
>>> str.replace("is","was")
'thwas was string example....wow!!! thwas was really string'
>>> str="this is string example....wow!!! this is really string"
>>> str.replace("is","was",3)
'thwas was string example....wow!!! thwas is really string'
```

The above can be imitated using `string` module's function `string.replace(s,old,new[,maxreplace])`, where s is a string and `maxreplace` is same as `count` (discussed above).

```
>>> str="this is string example....wow!!! this is really string"
>>> string.replace(str,"is","was")
'thwas was string example....wow!!! thwas was really string'
>>> str="this is string example....wow!!! this is really string"
>>> string.replace(str,"is","was",3)
'thwas was string example....wow!!! thwas is really string'
```

`str.center(width[,fillchar])`
Return centered string of length `width`. Padding is done using optional argument `fillchar` (default is a space).

```
>>> str="this is string example....wow!!!"
>>> str.center(40,'a')
'aaaathis is string example....wow!!!aaaa'
>>> str="this is string example....wow!!!"
>>> str.center(40)
'    this is string example....wow!!!    '
```

The above can be imitated using `string` module's function `string.center(s,width[,fillchar])`, where s is a string.

```
>>> str="this is string example....wow!!!"
>>> string.center(str,40,'a')
'aaaathis is string example....wow!!!aaaa'
>>> str="this is string example....wow!!!"
>>> string.center(str,40)
'    this is string example....wow!!!    '
```

`str.ljust(width[,fillchar])`
Return the string left justified in a string of length `width`. Padding is done using the optional argument `fillchar` (default is a space). The original string is returned if `width` is less than or equal to `len(str)`.

```
>>> str="this is string example....wow!!!"
>>> str.ljust(50,'0')
'this is string example....wow!!!00000000000000000000'
>>> str="this is string example....wow!!!"
>>> str.ljust(50)
'this is string example....wow!!!                  '
>>> str="this is string example....wow!!!"
>>> str.ljust(10)
'this is string example....wow!!!'
```

The above can be imitated using `string` module's function `string.ljust(s,width [,fillchar])`, where s is a string.

```
>>> str="this is string example....wow!!!"
>>> string.ljust(str,50,'0')
'this is string example....wow!!!00000000000000000000'
>>> str="this is string example....wow!!!"
>>> string.ljust(str,50)
'this is string example....wow!!!                  '
```

`str.rjust(width[,fillchar])`
Return the right justified string of length `width`. Padding is done using the optional argument `fillchar` (default is a space). The original string is returned if `width` is less than or equal to `len(str)`.

```
>>> str="this is string example....wow!!!"
>>> str.rjust(50,'0')
'00000000000000000this is string example....wow!!!'
>>> str="this is string example....wow!!!"
>>> str.rjust(10,'0')
'this is string example....wow!!!'
```

The above can be imitated using `string` module's function `string.rjust(s,width [,fillchar])`, where s is a string.

```
>>> str="this is string example....wow!!!"
>>> string.rjust(str,50,'0')
'00000000000000000this is string example....wow!!!'
>>> str="this is string example....wow!!!"
>>> string.rjust(str,10,'0')
'this is string example....wow!!!'
```

`str.zfill(width)`
Return a string of length `width`, having leading zeros. The original string is returned, if `width` is less than or equal to `len(str)`.

```
>>> str="this is string example....wow!!!"
>>> str.zfill(40)
```

```
'00000000this is string example....wow!!!'
>>> str.zfill(45)
'0000000000000this is string example....wow!!!'
```

The above can be imitated using `string` module's function `string.zfill(s,width)`, where `s` is a string.

```
>>> str="this is string example....wow!!!"
>>> string.zfill(str,40)
'00000000this is string example....wow!!!'
>>> string.zfill(str,45)
'0000000000000this is string example....wow!!!'
```

`str.strip([chars])`
Return a string with the leading and trailing characters removed. The `chars` argument is a string specifying the set of characters to be removed. If omitted or `None`, the `chars` argument defaults to removing whitespace.

```
>>> str="0000000this is string example....wow!!!0000000"
>>> str.strip('0')
'this is string example....wow!!!'
```

The above can be imitated using `string` module's function `string.strip(s[,chars])`, where `s` is a string.

```
>>> str="0000000this is string example....wow!!!0000000"
>>> string.strip(str,'0')
'this is string example....wow!!!'
```

`str.lstrip([chars])`
Return a string with leading characters removed. The `chars` argument is a string specifying the set of characters to be removed. If omitted or `None`, the `chars` argument defaults to removing whitespace.

```
>>> str="      this is string example....wow!!!        "
>>> str.lstrip()
'this is string example....wow!!!        '
>>> str="88888888this is string example....wow!!!8888888"
>>> str.lstrip('8')
'this is string example....wow!!!8888888'
```

The above can be imitated using `string` module's function `string.lstrip(s[,chars])`, where `s` is a string.

```
>>> str="      this is string example....wow!!!        "
>>> string.lstrip(str)
'this is string example....wow!!!        '
>>> str="88888888this is string example....wow!!!8888888"
>>> string.lstrip(str,'8')
```

```
'this is string example....wow!!!8888888'
```

`str.rstrip([chars])`

Return a string with trailing characters removed. The `chars` argument is a string specifying the set of characters to be removed. If omitted or `None`, the `chars` argument defaults to removing whitespace.

```
>>> str="     this is string example....wow!!!     "
>>> str.rstrip()
'     this is string example....wow!!!'
>>> str="88888888this is string example....wow!!!8888888"
>>> str.rstrip('8')
'88888888this is string example....wow!!!'
```

The above can be imitated using `string` module's function `string.rstrip(s[,chars])`, where `s` is a string.

```
>>> str="     this is string example....wow!!!     "
>>> string.rstrip(str)
'     this is string example....wow!!!'
>>> str="88888888this is string example....wow!!!8888888"
>>> string.rstrip(str,'8')
'88888888this is string example....wow!!!'
```

`str.partition(sep)`

Split the string at the first occurrence of `sep`, and return a tuple containing the part before the separator, the separator itself, and the part after the separator.

```
>>> str="     this is string example....wow!!!     "
>>> str.partition('s')
('     thi', 's', ' is string example....wow!!!     ')
```

`str.rpartition(sep)`

Split the string at the last occurrence of `sep`, and return a tuple containing the part before the separator, the separator itself, and the part after the separator.

```
>>> str="     this is string example....wow!!!     "
>>> str.rpartition('s')
('     this is ', 's', 'tring example....wow!!!     ')
```

`str.split([sep[,maxsplit]])`

Return a list of the words from the string using `sep` as the delimiter string. If `maxsplit` is given, at most `maxsplit` splits are done (thus, the list will have at most `maxsplit+1` elements). If `maxsplit` is not specified or -1, then all possible splits are made. If `sep` is not specified or `None`, any whitespace string is a separator.

```
>>> str="Line1-abcdef \nLine2-abc \nLine4-abcd"
>>> str.split()
['Line1-abcdef', 'Line2-abc', 'Line4-abcd']
```

```
>>> str.split(' ',1)
['Line1-abcdef', '\nLine2-abc \nLine4-abcd']
```

The above can be imitated using `string` module's function `string.split(s[,sep [,maxsplit]])`, where s is a string.

```
>>> str="Line1-abcdef \nLine2-abc \nLine4-abcd"
>>> string.split(str)
['Line1-abcdef', 'Line2-abc', 'Line4-abcd']
>>> string.split(str,' ',1)
['Line1-abcdef', '\nLine2-abc \nLine4-abcd']
```

`str.rsplit([sep[,maxsplit]])`
Return a list of the words from the string using `sep` as the delimiter string. If `maxsplit` is given, at most `maxsplit` splits are done, the rightmost ones. If `sep` is not specified or `None`, any whitespace string is a separator. Except for splitting from the right, `rsplit()` behaves like `split()` which is described in detail below.

```
>>> str="     this is string example....wow!!!      "
>>> str.rsplit()
['this', 'is', 'string', 'example....wow!!!']
>>> str.rsplit('s')
['     thi', ' i', ' ', 'tring example....wow!!!      ']
```

The above can be imitated using `string` module's function `string.rsplit(s[,sep [,maxsplit]])`, where s is a string.

```
>>> str="     this is string example....wow!!!      "
>>> string.rsplit(str)
['this', 'is', 'string', 'example....wow!!!']
>>> string.rsplit(str,'s')
['     thi', ' i', ' ', 'tring example....wow!!!      ']
```

`str.splitlines([keepends])`
Return a list of the lines in the string, breaking at line boundaries. Line breaks are not included in the resulting list unless `keepends` is given.

```
>>> str="Line1-a b c d e f\nLine2- a b c\n\nLine4- a b c d"
>>> str.splitlines()
['Line1-a b c d e f', 'Line2- a b c', '', 'Line4- a b c d']
>>> str.splitlines(0)
['Line1-a b c d e f', 'Line2- a b c', '', 'Line4- a b c d']
>>> str.splitlines(False)
['Line1-a b c d e f', 'Line2- a b c', '', 'Line4- a b c d']
>>> str.splitlines(1)
['Line1-a b c d e f\n', 'Line2- a b c\n', '\n', 'Line4- a b c d']
>>> str.splitlines(True)
['Line1-a b c d e f\n', 'Line2- a b c\n', '\n', 'Line4- a b c d']
```

`str.translate(table[,deletechars])`

Return a string having all characters occurring in the optional argument `deletechars` are removed, and the remaining characters have been mapped through the given translation table, which must be a string of length 256.

The `maketrans()` function (discussed later in this section) from the `string` module is used to create a translation table. For string objects, set the `table` argument to `None` for translations that only delete characters.

```
>>> str='this is string example....wow!!!!'
>>> tab=string.maketrans('e','E')
>>> str.translate(tab)
'this is string ExamplE....wow!!!!'
>>> str.translate(tab,'ir')
'ths s stng ExamplE....wow!!!!'
>>> str.translate(None,'ir')
'ths s stng example....wow!!!!'
```

The above can be imitated using `string` module's function `string.translate(s,table[,deletechars])`, where s is a string.

```
>>> str='this is string example....wow!!!!'
>>> tab=string.maketrans('e','E')
>>> string.translate(str,tab)
'this is string ExamplE....wow!!!!'
>>> string.translate(str,tab,'ir')
'ths s stng ExamplE....wow!!!!'
>>> string.translate(str,None,'ir')
'ths s stng example....wow!!!!'
```

The following functions are there in `string` module, but are not available as string methods.

`string.capwords(s[,sep])`

Split the argument s into words using `str.split()`, then capitalize each word using `str.capitalize()`, and join the capitalized words using `str.join()`. If the optional second argument `sep` is absent or `None`, runs of whitespace characters are replaced by a single space and leading and trailing whitespace are removed, otherwise, `sep` is used to split and join the words.

```
>>> str="   this is string example....   wow!!!    "
>>> string.capwords(str)
'This Is String Example.... Wow!!!'
>>> string.capwords(str,' ')
'   This Is String Example....   Wow!!!    '
>>> string.capwords(str,'s')
'   this is sTring example....   wow!!!    '
```

`string.maketrans(from,to)`

Return a translation table suitable for passing to `translate()`, that will map each character in `from` into the character at the same position in `to`, `from` and `to` must have the same length.

```
>>> str='this is string example....wow!!!'
>>> tab=string.maketrans('t!','T.')
>>> string.translate(str,tab)
'This is sTring example....wow...'
>>> string.translate(str,tab,'ir')
'Ths s sTng example....wow...'
>>> string.translate(str,None,'ir')
'ths s stng example....wow!!!'
```

2.10.4. Regular expression module

Regular expression (also called RE, or regex, or regex pattern) is a specialized approach in Python, using which programmer can specify rules for the set of possible strings that needs to be matched; this set might contain english sentences, e-mail addresses, or anything. REs can also be used to modify a string or to split it apart in various ways.

2.10.4.1. Meta characters

Most letters and characters will simply match themselves. For example, the regular expression `test` will match the string `test` exactly. There are exceptions to this rule; some characters are special "meta characters", and do not match themselves. Instead, they signal that some out-of-the-ordinary thing should be matched, or they affect other portions of the RE by repeating them or changing their meaning. Some of the meta characters are discussed below:

Table 2-14: Meta characters

Meta character	Description	Example
[ ]	Used to match a set of characters.	*[time]* The regular expression would match any of the characters *t, i, m* or *e*. *[a-z]* The regular expression would match only lowercase characters.
^	Used to complement a set of characters.	*[^time]* The regular expression would match any other characters than *t, i, m* or *e*.
$	Used to match the end of string only.	*time$* The regular expression would match *time* in *ontime*, but will not match *time* in *timetable*.
*	Used to specify that the previous character can be matched zero or more times.	*tim*e* The regular expression would match strings like *timme, tie* and so on.
+	Used to specify that the previous character can be matched one or more times.	*tim+e* The regular expression would match strings like *timme, timmme, time* and so on.

[52]

Meta character	Description	Example
?	Used to specify that the previous character can be matched either once or zero times.	*tim?e* The regular expression would only match strings like *time* or *tie*.
{}	The curly brackets accept two integer values. The first value specifies the minimum number of occurrences and second value specifies the maximum of occurrences.	*tim{1,4}e* The regular expression would match only strings *time*, *timme*, *timmme* or *timmmme*.

2.10.4.2. Regular expression module functions

Some of the methods of re module as discussed below:

`re.compile(pattern)`
The function compile a regular expression pattern into a regular expression object, which can be used for matching using its `match()` and `search()` methods, discussed below.

```
>>> import re
>>> p=re.compile('tim*e')
```

`re.match(pattern,string)`
If zero or more characters at the beginning of `string` match the regular expression `pattern`, `match()` return a corresponding `MatchObject` instance. The function returns `None`, if the string does not match the pattern.

`re.group()`
The function return the string matched by the RE.

```
>>> m=re.match('tim*e','timme pass time')
>>> m.group()
'timme'
```

The above patch of code can also be written as:

```
>>> p=re.compile('tim*e')
>>> m=p.match('timme pass timme')
>>> m.group()
'timme'
```

`re.search(pattern,string)`
The function scans through `string` looking for a location where the regular expression `pattern` produces a match, and return a corresponding `MatchObject` instance. The function returns `None`, if no position in the string matches the pattern.

```
>>> m=re.search('tim*e','no passtimmmeee')
>>> m.group()
'timmme'
```

The above patch of code can also be written as:

```
>>> p=re.compile('tim*e')
>>> m=p.search('no passtimmmeee')
>>> m.group()
'timmme'
```

`re.start()`
The function returns the starting position of the match.

`re.end()`
The function returns the end position of the match.

`re.span()`
The function returns a tuple containing the `(start,end)` indexes of the match.

```
>>> m=re.search('tim*e','no passtimmmeee')
>>> m.start()
7
>>> m.end()
13
>>> m.span()
(7, 13)
```

The above patch of code can also be written as:

```
>>> p=re.compile('tim*e')
>>> m=p.search('no passtimmmeee')
>>> m.start()
7
>>> m.end()
13
>>> m.span()
(7, 13)
```

`re.findall(pattern,string)`
The function returns all non-overlapping matches of `pattern` in `string`, as a list of strings. The `string` is scanned left-to-right, and matches are returned in the order found.

```
>>> m=re.findall('tim*e','timeee break no pass timmmeee')
>>> m
['time', 'timmme']
```

The above patch of code can also be written as:

```
>>> p=re.compile('tim*e')
>>> m=p.findall('timeee break no pass timmmeee')
>>> m
['time', 'timmme']
```

`re.finditer(pattern,string)`
The function returns an iterator yielding `MatchObject` instances over all non-overlapping matches for the RE `pattern` in `string`. The `string` is scanned left-to-right, and matches are returned in the order found.

```
>>> m=re.finditer('tim*e','timeee break no pass timmmeee')
>>> for match in m:
...      print match.group()
...      print match.span()
...
time
(0, 4)
timmme
(21, 27)
```

The above patch of code can also be written as:

```
>>> p=re.compile('tim*e')
>>> m=p.finditer('timeee break no pass timmmeee')
>>> for match in m:
...      print match.group()
...      print match.span()
...
time
(0, 4)
timmme
(21, 27)
```

2.11. Error

An error (or software bug) is a fault in a computer program that produces incorrect or unexpected result, or causes it to behave in unintended ways. Mostly bug arise from mistakes and errors made by people in either a program's source code or its design. Usually, errors are classified as: syntax error, run-time error and logical error.

2.11.1. Syntax error

Syntax error refers to an error in the syntax of tokens and/or sequence of tokens that is intended to be written in a particular programming language. For compiled languages, syntax errors occur strictly at compile-time. A program will not compile until all syntax errors are corrected. For interpreted languages, however, not all syntax errors can be reliably detected until run-time.

```
>>> prin 'Hi'
SyntaxError: invalid syntax
```

```
>>> print "Hi'
SyntaxError: EOL while scanning string literal
```

2.11.2. Run-time error

Run-time error is an error which can be detected during the execution of a program. The code appears to be correct (it has no syntax errors), but it will not execute. For example, if a programmer has written a correct code to open a file using `open()` function, and if the file is corrupted, the application cannot carry out the execution of `open()` function, and it stops running.

2.11.3. Logical error

Logical error (or semantic error) is a bug in a program that causes it to operate incorrectly, but not terminate abnormally. A logical error produces unintended or undesired output or other behavior, although it may not immediately be recognized. Logic error occurs both in compiled and interpreted languages. Unlike a program with a syntax error, a program with a logical error is a valid program in the language, though it does not behave as intended. The only clue to the existence of logic errors is the production of wrong solutions. For example, if a program calculates average of variables a and b, instead of writing the expression $c=(a+b)/2$, one can write $c=a+b/2$, which is a logical error.

```
>>> print a+b/2
6.5
>>> print (a+b)/2
5.0
```

Chapter 3
SIMPLE AND COMPOUND STATEMENTS

A statement is a unit of code that the Python interpreter can execute. A script usually contains a sequence of statements.

Namespace is a logical grouping of the objects used within a program. Most namespaces are currently implemented as Python dictionaries. Examples of namespaces are the set of built-in names (containing functions such as `abs()`, and built-in exception names), the global names in a module, and the local names in a function definition. The important thing to know about namespace is that there is absolutely no relation between names in different namespaces. For instance, the functions `__builtin__.open()` and `os.open()` are distinguished by their namespaces. The following is an example of local namespace.

```
>>> def example(arg):
...     x=4
...     print locals()
...
>>> example(10)
{'x': 4, 'arg': 10}
>>> example('hello')
{'x': 4, 'arg': 'hello'}
```

The function `example()` has two variables in its local namespace: `arg`, whose value is passed in to the function, and `x`, which is defined within the function. The `locals()` built-in function return a dictionary of name-value pairs; the keys of this dictionary are the names of local variables as strings; the values of the dictionary are the actual values of the variables.

3.1.   Simple statement
Simple statement is comprised within a single logical line. Several simple statements may occur on a single physical line separated by semicolons. The extended BNF notation describing syntax for simple statement is:

```
simple_stmt ::=  expression_stmt
                | assert_stmt
                | assignment_stmt
                | augmented_assignment_stmt
                | pass_stmt
                | del_stmt
                | print_stmt
                | return_stmt
                | yield_stmt
                | raise_stmt
                | break_stmt
                | continue_stmt
```

```
            | import_stmt
            | global_stmt
            | exec_stmt
```

This book will discuss some of the simple statements.

3.1.1. Expression statement

An expression in a programming language is a combination of values, constants, variables, operators, functions etc. that are interpreted according to the particular rules of precedence for a particular programming language, which computes and then return another value. This process is called evaluation. An expression statement evaluates the expression list (which may be a single expression).

```
expression_stmt ::=  expression_list
```

The following are examples of expression statement and its evaluation.

```
>>> 4
4
>>> 4==4
True
>>> 2+6
8
>>> 'Hi'*3
'HiHiHi'
```

3.1.2. Assignment statement

Assignment statements are used to (re)bind names to values and to modify attributes or items of mutable objects. The following example shows binding value 4 to object (or name) `a`.

```
>>> a=4
```

3.1.3. Pass statement

The pass statement is a null operation, nothing happens when it is executed. It is useful as a placeholder when a statement is required syntactically, but no code needs to be executed.

```
pass_stmt ::=  "pass"
```

The following example defines a function `f` and does nothing.

```
>>> def f(arg):
...      pass
...
```

3.1.4. Del statement

This statement deletes each target in `target_list` from left to right.

```
del_stmt ::=  "del" target_list
```

Deletion of a name removes the binding of that name from the local or global namespace, depending on whether the name occurs in a `global` statement in the same code block. If the name is unbound, a `NameError` exception will be raised.

```
>>> a = [-1, 1, 66.25, 333, 333, 1234.5]
>>> del a[0]
>>> a
[1, 66.25, 333, 333, 1234.5]
>>> del a[2:4]
>>> a
[1, 66.25, 1234.5]
>>> del a[:]
>>> a
[]
>>> a = [-1, 1, 66.25, 333, 333, 1234.5]
>>> del a
>>> a

Traceback (most recent call last):
  File "<pyshell#24>", line 1, in <module>
    a
NameError: name 'a' is not defined
```

3.1.5. Print statement

The `print` statement evaluates each expression and then writes the resulting object to standard output (computer screen). If an object is not a string, it is first converted to a string using the rules for string conversion, the resulting or original string is then written. A space is written before each object is (converted and) written, unless the output system believes it is positioned at the beginning of a line. A `'\n'` character is written at the end, unless the `print` statement ends with a comma. If only `print` keyword is there in `print` statement, then only `'\n'` character is written. Following is a script "print_example.py", having the following code:

```
a=20
print 'hi',5,a
print 'bye',10,a
print
print 'hi',5,a,
print 'bye',10,a,
```

Output after running the script is:

```
>>> runfile('C:/Temp/print_example.py', wdir=r'C:/Temp')
hi 5 20
bye 10 20

hi 5 20 bye 10 20
```

3.1.6.   Return statement

The `return` statement leaves the current function call with the `expression_list` (or `None`) as return value.

```
return_stmt ::=  "return" [expression_list]
```

The following script "addition_example.py" demonstrate the use of return statement.

```
def summation(arg1,arg2):
    return arg1+arg2

print 'Sum is: ',summation(1,2)

def summation(arg1,arg2):              # The function return None
    print 'Sum is: ',arg1+arg2

summation(3,4)
print summation(3,4)

def summation(arg1,arg2):              # The function return None
    print 'Sum is: ',arg1+arg2
    return

summation(5,6)
print summation(5,6)

def summation(arg1,arg2):              # The function return None
    print 'Sum is: ',arg1+arg2
    return None

summation(7,8)
print summation(7,8)

def summation(arg1,arg2):
    def add(arg1,arg2):
        return arg1+arg2
    return add(arg1,arg2)

print 'Sum is: ',summation(9,10)
```

The output after running the script is:

```
>>> runfile('C:/Temp/addition_example.py', wdir=r'C:/Temp')
Sum is:  3
Sum is:  7
Sum is:  7
None
Sum is:  11
Sum is:  11
```

```
None
Sum is:    15
Sum is:    15
None
Sum is:    19
```

3.1.7. Break statement

The `break` statement terminate the nearest enclosing loop, skipping the optional `else` clause if the loop has one.

```
break_stmt ::=   "break"
```

If a `for` loop is terminated by `break`, the loop control target keeps its current value. The following script "break_example.py" demonstrates the use of `break` statement.

```
a=5
for i in range(10):
    if i==a:
        break
    else:
        print i

print i
```

The output after running the script is:

```
>>> runfile('C:/Temp/addition_example.py', wdir=r'C:/Temp')
0
1
2
3
4
5
```

3.1.8. Continue statement

The `continue` statement makes the current nearest enclosing loop to skip one iteration and executes the remaining ones.

```
continue_stmt ::=   "continue"
```

The following script "continue_example.py" demonstrate the use of `continue` statement.

```
for i in range(10):
    if i>4 and i<8:
        continue
    else:
        print i
```

The output after running the script is:

```
>>> runfile('C:/Temp/continue_example.py', wdir=r'C:/Temp')
0
1
2
3
4
8
9
```

3.1.9. Import statement
Definitions (variables, function definitions etc.) from one module can be imported into other module using `import` statement. For more information, please refer chapter 5.

3.1.10. Global statement
The `global` statement is a declaration which makes listed identifiers to be interpreted as global. This will become clearer by referring section 3.2.5.

```
global_stmt ::= "global" identifier ("," identifier)*
```

3.2. Compound statement
Compound statements contain groups of other statements, they affect or control the execution of those other statements in some way. In general, compound statements span multiple lines, although a whole compound statement can be contained in one line.

The `if`, `while` and `for` statements are the traditional control flow compound statements. `try` specifies exception handlers and/or cleanup code for a group of statements. Function and class definitions are also syntactically compound statements.

Compound statements consist of one or more clauses. A clause consists of a header and a suite. The clause headers of a particular compound statement are all at the same indentation level. Each clause header begin with a uniquely identifying keyword and ends with a colon. A suite is a group of statements controlled by a clause. A suite can be one or more semicolon-separated simple statements on the same line as the header, following the header's colon, or it can be one or more indented statements on subsequent lines. Only the latter form of suite can contain nested compound statements.

The colon is required primarily to enhance readability.

```
if a == b
    print aversus

if a == b:
    print a
```

Notice how the second one is slightly easier to read. Another minor reason is that the colon makes it easier for editors with syntax highlighting; they can look for colons to decide when indentation needs to be increased.

A code block (or simply "block") is a piece of Python program text that is executed as a unit. Few examples of block are: a module, a function body, a class definition etc. Each command typed interactively is a block.

3.2.1. If statement

The `if` statement is used for conditional execution:

```
if_stmt ::=   "if" expression ":" suite
              ( "elif" expression ":" suite )*
              ["else" ":" suite]
```

It selects exactly one of the suites by evaluating the expressions one by one until one is found to be true, then that suite is executed (and no other part of the `if` statement is executed or evaluated). If all expressions are false, the suite of the `else` clause (if present) is executed.

```
>>> var=100
>>> if var==100:
...     print 'var has value 100'
...
var has value 100
>>>
>>> var=100
>>> if var<>100:
...     print 'var does not have value 100'
... else:
...     print 'var has value 100'
...
var has value 100
>>>
>>> var=100
>>> if var<100:
...     print 'var has value less than 100'
... elif var>100:
...     print 'var has value greater than 100'
... else:
...     print 'var has value 100'
...
var has value 100
```

The following example shows that if the evaluation of expression gives result either `None`, empty string (`' '`), zero (0) or Boolean `False`, then the condition is considered as false.

```
>>> if None or '' or 0 or False:
...     print 'Atleast one condition is true'
```

```
... else:
...      print 'None of the condition is true'
...
None of the condition is true
```

There may be a situation when there is a need to check for another condition after a condition resolves to true. In such a situation, the nested `if` statement can be used.

```
>>> var=100
>>> if isinstance(var,str):
...      print 'var is a string'
... elif (type(var) is int):
...      if var<>100:
...          print 'var does not have value 100'
...      else:
...          print 'var has value 100'
...
var has value 100
```

3.2.2.   While statement

The `while` statement is used for repeated execution of group of statements as long as an expression is true:

```
while_stmt ::=   "while" expression ":" suite
                 ["else" ":" suite]
```

This compound statement repeatedly tests the expression, and if it is true, it executes the first suite; if the expression is false (which may be the first time it is tested) the suite of the `else` clause (if present) is executed and the loop terminates.

```
>>> var=1
>>> while var<=5:
...      print 'Count ',var
...      var=var+1
...
Count   1
Count   2
Count   3
Count   4
Count   5
>>> print 'The loop ends'
The loop ends
```

The above code can also be witten as follows:

```
>>> var=1
>>> while var<=5:
...      print 'Count ',var
```

```
...        var=var+1
... else:
...        print 'The loop ends'
...
Count    1
Count    2
Count    3
Count    4
Count    5
The loop ends
```

A `break` statement executed in the first suite terminates the loop without executing the `else` clause's suite.

```
>>> var=1
>>> while var<=5:
...        print 'Count ',var
...        var=var+1
...        if var==4:
...             break
... else:
...        print 'The loop ends'
...
Count    1
Count    2
Count    3
```

A `continue` statement executed in the first suite skips the rest of the suite and goes back to testing the expression.

```
>>> var=0
>>> while var<=5:
...        var=var+1
...        if var>=3 and var<=4:
...             continue
...        print 'Count ',var
...
Count    1
Count    2
Count    5
Count    6
```

Consider a scenario where the condition never becomes false. This results in a loop that never ends; such loop is called an infinite loop. One needs to use keyboard *Ctrl+C* to come out of the program.

3.2.3. For statement

The `for` statement is used to iterate over the elements of a sequence (such as a string, tuple or list) or other iterable object:

```
for_stmt ::=    "for" target_list "in" expression_list ":" suite
                ["else" ":" suite]
```

The expression list `expression_list` is evaluated once; it should yield an iterable object. An iterator is created for the result of the `expression_list`. The suite is then executed once for each item provided by the iterator, in the order of ascending indices. Each item in turn is assigned to the target list `target_list` using the standard rules for assignments, and then the suite is executed. When the items are exhausted (which is immediately when the sequence is empty), the suite in the `else` clause (if present) is executed, and the loop terminates.

```
>>> for i in [1,2,3,4,5]:
...       print 'Count ',i
...
Count  1
Count  2
Count  3
Count  4
Count  5
>>> print 'The loop ends'
The loop ends
```

The above code can also be witten as follows:

```
>>> for i in range(1,6):
...       print 'Count ',i
... else:
...       print 'The loop ends'
...
Count  1
Count  2
Count  3
Count  4
Count  5
The loop ends
```

A `break` statement executed in the first suite terminates the loop without executing the `else` clause's suite.

```
>>> for i in [1,2,3,4,5]:
...       if i==4:
...            break
...       print 'Count ',i
... else:
...       print 'The loop ends'
...
Count  1
Count  2
```

```
Count  3
```

A `continue` statement executed in the first suite skips the rest of the suite and continues with the next item, or with the `else` clause if there was no next item.

```
>>> for i in [1,2,3,4,5]:
...      if i==4:
...          continue
...      print 'Count ',i
... else:
...      print 'The loop ends'
...
Count  1
Count  2
Count  3
Count  5
The loop ends
```

There might be scenario where one needs to print the item along with its index. The following example demonstrate this scenario using `enumerate()` built-in function (discussed later in this chapter).

```
>>> shuttles=['columbia','endeavour','challenger']
>>> for index,value in enumerate(shuttles):
...      print index, value
...
0 columbia
1 endeavour
2 challenger
>>>
>>> value
'challenger'
>>> index
2
```

It can also be observed that the target list is not deleted when the loop is finished.

3.2.4. Functions

Function is a compound statement which returns some value to the caller. The keyword `def` introduces a function definition. It must be followed by the function name and the parenthesized list of formal parameters. The statements that form the body of the function start at the next line, and must be indented. The first statement of the function body can optionally be a string literal; this string literal is the function's documentation string, or "docstring". Docstring is a string literal which appears as the first expression in a class, function or module. While ignored when the suite is executed, it is recognized by the compiler and put into the __doc__ attribute of the enclosing class, function or module.

```
>>> def summation(a,b):
...      """ Gives sum of
```

```
...             two numbers"""
...          sum=a+b
...          return sum
...
>>> summation(5,10)
15
>>> summation.__doc__
' Gives sum of\n          two numbers'
```

3.2.4.1. Argument

Argument is the value passed to a function (or method) while calling the function. There are two types of arguments:

3.2.4.1.1. Keyword argument

Keyword argument is an argument preceded by an identifier (e.g. `name=`) in a function call or passed as a value in a dictionary preceded by **. For example, 10, 20, 30 and 40 are keyword arguments in the following calls to `summation()` function:

```
>>> def summation(aa,bb,cc,dd):
...          print 'aa:',aa
...          print 'bb:',bb
...          print 'cc:',cc
...          print 'dd:',dd
...          total=aa+bb+cc+dd
...          return total
...
>>> sumup1=summation(bb=20,dd=40,aa=10,cc=30)
aa: 10
bb: 20
cc: 30
dd: 40
>>> print 'Sum is:',sumup1
Sum is: 100
>>> sumup2=summation(**{'bb':20,'dd':40,'aa':10,'cc':30})
aa: 10
bb: 20
cc: 30
dd: 40
>>> print 'Sum is:',sumup2
Sum is: 100
```

3.2.4.1.2. Positional argument

Positional argument is an argument that is not a keyword argument. Positional arguments can appear at the beginning of an argument list and can also be passed as elements of an iterable preceded by *. For example, 10, 20, 30 and 40 are positional arguments in the following calls to `summation()` function:

```
>>> def summation(aa,bb,cc,dd):
```

[68]

```
...        print 'aa:',aa
...        print 'bb:',bb
...        print 'cc:',cc
...        print 'dd:',dd
...        total=aa+bb+cc+dd
...        return total
...
>>> sumup3=summation(10,20,30,40)
aa: 10
bb: 20
cc: 30
dd: 40
>>> print 'Sum is:',sumup3
Sum is: 100
>>> sumup4=summation(*(10,20,30,40))
aa: 10
bb: 20
cc: 30
dd: 40
>>> print 'Sum is:',sumup4
Sum is: 100
```

3.2.4.2. Parameter

Parameter is a named entity in a function (or method) definition that specifies the argument (or in some cases, arguments), that the function can accept. Parameters are defined by the names that appear in a function definition, whereas arguments are the values actually passed to a function when calling it. For example, given the function definition:

```
def func(foo,bar=None,**kwargs):
    pass
```

`foo`, `bar` and `kwargs` are parameters of `func`. However, when calling `func`, for example:

```
func(42,bar=314,extra=somevar)
```

the values 42, 314, and `somevar` are arguments.

The actual parameters (arguments) to a function call are introduced in the local symbol table of the called function when it is called; thus, arguments are passed using call by value (where the value is always an object reference, not the value of the object). Actually, call by object reference would be a better description, since if a mutable object is passed, the caller will see any changes the callee makes to it (items inserted into a list).

```
>>> def changeme(mylist):
...        mylist.append([1,2,3,4])
...        print "Values inside the function: ",mylist
...        return
...
```

```
>>> mylist=[10,20,30]
>>> changeme(mylist)
Values inside the function:  [10, 20, 30, [1, 2, 3, 4]]
>>> print "Values outside the function: ",mylist
Values outside the function:  [10, 20, 30, [1, 2, 3, 4]]
```

In the above example, the append operation maintains the passed object reference. In the following example the object reference is overwritten inside the function.

```
>>> def changeme(mylist):
...       mylist=[1,2,3,4]
...       print "Values inside the function: ",mylist
...       return
...
>>> mylist=[10,20,30]
>>> changeme(mylist)
Values inside the function:  [1, 2, 3, 4]
>>> print "Values outside the function: ",mylist
Values outside the function:  [10, 20, 30]
```

There are four types of parameters:

3.2.4.2.1. Positional or keyword parameter
It specifies that an argument can be passed either positionally or as a keyword argument. Note that, only those parameters which are at the end of the parameter list can be given default argument values i.e. the function cannot have a parameter with a default argument value preceding a parameter without a default argument value in the function's parameter list. This is because the values are assigned to the parameters by position. For example, `def func(a,b=5)` is valid, but `def func(a=5,b)` is not valid.

3.2.4.2.2. Only positional parameter
It specifies that an argument that can be supplied only by position.

3.2.4.2.3. Var-positional parameter
It specifies that an arbitrary sequence of positional arguments can be provided (in addition to any positional arguments already accepted by other parameters). Such a parameter can be defined by prepending the parameter name with *.

3.2.4.2.4. Var-keyword parameter
It specifies that arbitrarily many keyword arguments can be provided (in addition to any keyword arguments already accepted by other parameters). Such a parameter can be defined by prefixing the parameter name with **.

Following are few examples of functions.

```
>>> def person_info(fn,ln,ag,tel=5128975,nat='American'):
...       print 'First name:',fn
```

```
...        print 'Last name:',ln
...        print 'Age:',ag
...        print 'Telephone number:',tel
...        print 'Nationality:',nat
...
>>> person_info('Sachin','Tendulkar',40,17896823,'Indian')
First name: Sachin
Last name: Tendulkar
Age: 40
Telephone number: 17896823
Nationality: Indian
>>> person_info('Mike','Johnson',20)
First name: Mike
Last name: Johnson
Age: 20
Telephone number: 5128975
Nationality: American
>>> person_info('Nadeem','Khan',54,nat='Pakistani')
First name: Nadeem
Last name: Khan
Age: 54
Telephone number: 5128975
Nationality: Pakistani
>>> person_info('Chin','Chan',15,nat='Chinese',tel=1894313654)
First name: Chin
Last name: Chan
Age: 15
Telephone number: 1894313654
Nationality: Chinese
>>>
>>> def person_info(fn,ln,ag,tel,nat):
...        print 'First name:',fn
...        print 'Last name:',ln
...        print 'Age:',ag
...        print 'Telephone number:',tel
...        print 'Nationality:',nat
...
>>> person_info('Sachin','Tendulkar',40,17896823,'Indian')
First name: Sachin
Last name: Tendulkar
Age: 40
Telephone number: 17896823
Nationality: Indian
>>> person_info('Chin','Chan',15,1894313654,'Chinese')
First name: Chin
Last name: Chan
Age: 15
Telephone number: 1894313654
Nationality: Chinese
>>>
```

```
>>> def total(a,b,*numbers):
...     tot=a+b
...     for num in numbers:
...         tot=tot+num
...     return tot
...
>>> print 'Total:',total(1,2,3,4,5)
Total: 15
>>> print 'Total:',total(1,2,3,4,5,6,7,8,9,10)
Total: 55
>>>
>>> def person_info(fn='Chin',ln='Chan',**more_info):
...     print 'First name:',fn
...     print 'Last name:',ln
...     if more_info.has_key('ag'):
...         print 'Age:',more_info['ag']
...     if more_info.has_key('tel'):
...         print 'Telephone number:',more_info['tel']
...     if more_info.has_key('nat'):
...         print 'Nationality:',more_info['nat']
...
>>> person_info()
First name: Chin
Last name: Chan
>>>  person_info(ag=40,tel=1789,ln='Tendulkar',nat='Indian',fn='Sachin
')
First name: Sachin
Last name: Tendulkar
Age: 40
Telephone number: 1789
Nationality: Indian
>>> person_info(ag=15,nat='Chinese',tel=1894313654)
First name: Chin
Last name: Chan
Age: 15
Telephone number: 1894313654
Nationality: Chinese
>>>
>>> def total(a,b,*numbers,**kwag):
...     tot=a+b
...     for num in numbers:
...         tot=tot+num
...     for key in kwag:
...         tot=tot+kwag[key]
...     return tot
...
>>> print 'Total:',total(5,7,10,2,14,c=100,d=106,e=211)
Total: 455
```

3.2.4.3.   Built-in functions

Till now, the discussed functions need to be defined before using it in program; such functions are called user-defined functions. Python has a number of functions that are always available. These are called built-in functions. They are listed here in alphabetical order.

abs()	all()	any()
basestring()	bin()	bool()
bytearray()	callable()	chr()
classmethod()	cmp()	compile()
complex()	delattr()	dict()
dir()	divmod()	enumerate()
eval()	execfile()	file()
filter()	float()	format()
frozenset()	getattr()	globals()
hasattr()	hash()	help()
hex()	id()	input()
int()	isinstance()	issubclass()
iter()	len()	list()
locals()	long()	map()
max()	memoryview()	min()
next()	object()	oct()
open()	ord()	pow()
print()	property()	range()
raw_input()	reduce()	reload()
repr()	reversed()	round()
set()	setattr()	slice()
sorted()	staticmethod()	str()
sum()	super()	tuple()
type()	unichr()	unicode()
vars()	xrange()	zip()
__import__()	apply()	buffer()
coerce()	intern()	

Some of the above built-in functions are discussed below:

`abs(x)`
Return the absolute value of a number. The argument may be a plain or long integer or a floating point number. If the argument is a complex number, its magnitude is returned.

```
>>> abs(-34)
34
>>> abs(34.5)
34.5
>>> abs(-3-4j)
5.0
```

`all(iterable)`
Return `True`, if all elements of the iterable are true (or if the iterable is empty).

[73]

```
>>> all([True,10])
True
>>> all([True,10,0])
False
>>> all(())
True
```

`any(iterable)`
Return `True`, if any element of the iterable is true. If the iterable is empty, return `False`.

```
>>> any([0,5,-3])
True
>>> any([0,False,-3])
True
>>> any(())
False
```

`bin(x)`
Convert an integer number to a binary string.

```
>>> bin(8)
'0b1000'
>>> bin(27)
'0b11011'
>>> (27).bit_length()
5
>>> bin(-1327)
'-0b10100101111'
>>> (-1327).bit_length()
11
```

`bool([x])`
Convert a value to a boolean. If x is false or omitted, this returns `False`; otherwise it returns `True`. If no argument is given, this function returns `False`.

```
>>> bool(5)
True
>>> bool(-5)
True
>>> bool(0)
False
>>> bool('hi')
True
>>> bool()
False
>>> bool('')
False
>>> bool(None)
```

```
False
>>> bool('\n')
True
>>> bool([0])
True
>>> bool((None,))
True
```

chr(i)

Return a string of one character whose ASCII-8 code is the integer i. This is the inverse of ord(). The argument must be in the range [0,255]; ValueError will be raised, if i is outside that range.

```
>>> for i in range(33,95): print i,'=',chr(i)
...
33 = !
34 = "
35 = #
36 = $
37 = %
38 = &
39 = '
40 = (
41 = )
42 = *
43 = +
44 = ,
45 = -
46 = .
47 = /
48 = 0
49 = 1
50 = 2
51 = 3
52 = 4
53 = 5
54 = 6
55 = 7
56 = 8
57 = 9
58 = :
59 = ;
60 = <
61 = =
62 = >
63 = ?
64 = @
65 = A
66 = B
67 = C
```

```
68 = D
69 = E
70 = F
71 = G
72 = H
73 = I
74 = J
75 = K
76 = L
77 = M
78 = N
79 = O
80 = P
81 = Q
82 = R
83 = S
84 = T
85 = U
86 = V
87 = W
88 = X
89 = Y
90 = Z
91 = [
92 = \
93 = ]
94 = ^
```

cmp(x,y)

Compare the two objects x and y, and return an integer according to the outcome. The returned value is negative, if x<y, zero, if x==y, and strictly positive, if x>y.

```
>>> cmp(2.5,5.2)
-1
>>> cmp(5.2,5.2)
0
>>> cmp(5.2,2.5)
1
>>> cmp('hi','hello')
1
>>> cmp('hello','hi')
-1
```

complex([real[,imag]])

Create a complex number with the value real+imag*j, or convert a string or number to a complex number. If the first parameter is a string, it will be interpreted as a complex number and the function must be called without a second parameter. The second parameter can never be a string. Each argument may be any numeric type (including complex). If imag is omitted, it defaults to zero. If both arguments are omitted, the function returns 0j. When converting from a string, the string must not contain whitespace around the central + or − operator. For example, `complex('1+2j')` is fine, but `complex('1 + 2j')` raises `ValueError`.

```
>>> complex()
0j
>>> complex(2.51)
(2.51+0j)
>>> complex(2.51,4.79)
(2.51+4.79j)
>>> c1=4+5j
>>> c2=6+7j
>>> complex(c1,c2) # Equals (4+5j)+(6+7j)j = 4+5j+6j-7
(-3+11j)
>>> c='7'
>>> complex(c)
(7+0j)
>>> c='7+4j'
>>> complex(c)
(7+4j)
>>> x=2+3j
>>> x.real
2.0
>>> x.imag
3.0
```

`delattr(object,name)`
This is a relative of `setattr()`. The arguments are an object and a string. The string must be the name of one of the object's attributes. The function deletes the named attribute, provided the `object` allows it.

```
>>> class new_cls:
...       def __init__(self,x):
...             self.x=x
...
>>> tt=new_cls(10)
>>> tt.x
10
>>> setattr(tt,'x',20)
>>> tt.x
20
>>> setattr(tt,'y','hello')
>>> tt.y
'hello'
>>> delattr(tt,'x')
>>> tt.x
Traceback (most recent call last):
  File "<stdin>", line 1, in <module>
AttributeError: new_cls instance has no attribute 'x'
```

```
divmod(a,b)
```
Take two (non-complex) numbers as arguments and return a pair of numbers consisting of their quotient and remainder.

```
>>> divmod(13.5,3)
(4.0, 1.5)
>>> divmod(13,3)
(4, 1)
```

```
enumerate(sequence,start=0)
```
Return an `enumerate` object. The `sequence` argument must be a sequence, an iterator, or some other object which supports iteration, while `start` is a count (default argument as 0).

```
>>> seasons=['Spring','Summer','Fall','Winter']
>>> list(enumerate(seasons))
[(0, 'Spring'), (1, 'Summer'), (2, 'Fall'), (3, 'Winter')]
>>> list(enumerate(seasons,start=2))
[(2, 'Spring'), (3, 'Summer'), (4, 'Fall'), (5, 'Winter')]
>>> for num,seasn in enumerate(seasons,start=1):
...        print "[{0}] {1}".format(num,seasn)
...
[1] Spring
[2] Summer
[3] Fall
[4] Winter
```

```
filter(function,iterable)
```
Create a list from those elements of `iterable` for which `function` returns `True`. The `iterable` may be either a sequence, a container which supports iteration, or an iterator. If `iterable` is a string or a tuple, the result also has that type, otherwise it will be a list. If `function` is `None`, the identity function is assumed, that is, all elements of `iterable` that are `False` are removed.

```
>>> def isOdd(x):
...        if(x%2)==1: return True
...        else: return False
...
>>> filter(isOdd,[88,43,65,-11,202])
[43, 65, -11]
>>>
>>> def isLetter(c): return c.isalpha()
...
>>> filter(isLetter,"01234abcdeFGHIJ*(&!^")
'abcdeFGHIJ'
>>> list=[0,1,(),(2,),0.0,0.25]
>>> filter(None,list)
[1, (2,), 0.25]
>>> filter(bool,list)
[1, (2,), 0.25]
```

```
getattr(object,name[,default])
```
Return the value of the named attribute of `object`; `name` must be a string. If the string is the name of one of the object's attributes, the result is the value of that attribute. If the named attribute does not exist, `default` is returned if provided, otherwise `AttributeError` is raised. For example, a complex number object has `real` and `imag` attributes.

```
>>> a=3.5+4.9J
>>> type(a)
<type 'complex'>
>>> getattr(a,'real')
3.5
>>> getattr(a,'imag')
4.9
>>> getattr(a,'imagine',2.2)
2.2
```

```
globals()
```
Return a dictionary representing the current global symbol table. The following script "GlobalScope.py" gives some idea about the use of this function.

```
# Filemame: GlobalScope.py
var1=10
def func():
    var2=20
func()
if 'var1' in globals().keys():
    print "'var1' is a global variable of this module"
if 'var2' in globals().keys():
    print "'var2' is a global variable of this module"
```

The output is:

```
'var1' is a global variable of this module
```

```
hasattr(object,name)
```
The arguments are an object and a string. The result is `True`, if the string is the name of one of the object's attributes, otherwise `False`.

```
>>> a=3.5+4.9J
>>> hasattr(a,'imag')
True
>>> hasattr(a,'imagine')
False
```

```
hash()
```
In computing, a hash table (also "hash map") is a data structure that can map keys to values. A hash table uses a hash function to compute an index (or hash value) into an array of buckets or slots, from

which the correct value can be found. The built-in function `hash()` return the hash value of the object (if it has one) which is basically an integer and it never changes during its lifetime.

Hashability makes an object usable as a dictionary key and a set member, because these data structures use the hash value internally. All of Python's immutable built-in objects are hashable, while no mutable containers (such as lists or dictionaries) are hashable.

```
>>> d={'Lisa':88.5,'John':69.73,'Mike':88.5}
>>> hash(d['Lisa'])
1485012992
>>> hash(d['John'])
-1664573625
>>> hash(d['Mike'])
1485012992
```

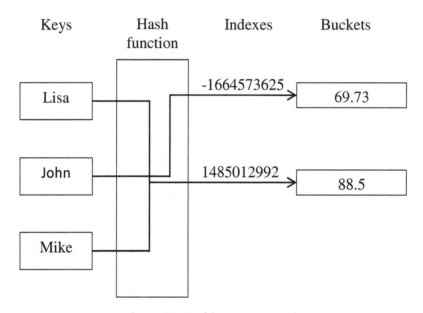

Figure 3-1: Hashing representation

Consider the following example:

```
>>> map(hash, ("namea","nameb","namec","named"))
[-1658398457, -1658398460, -1658398459, -1658398462]
>>> map(hash, (0,1,2,3))
[0, 1, 2, 3]
```

It can be observed that the strings are quite close in their letters, and their hashes are close in terms of numerical distance which is a desirable behaviour. If the keys are close in nature, one wants their hashes to be close as well so that lookups remain fast. Integers have same hash value as itself.

```
help([object])
```
This function invokes the built-in help system (this function is intended for interactive use). If no argument is given, the interactive help system starts on the interpreter console. If the argument is a

string, then the string is looked up as the name of a module, function, class, method, keyword, or documentation topic, and a help page is printed on the console. If the argument is any other kind of object, a help page on the object is generated.

```
>>> help(cmp)
Help on built-in function cmp in module __builtin__:

cmp(...)
    cmp(x, y) -> integer

    Return negative if x<y, zero if x==y, positive if x>y.
```

hex(x)
Convert an integer number (of any size) to a hexadecimal string. To obtain a hexadecimal string representation for a float, use the float.hex() method.

```
>>> hex(25)
'0x19'
```

id(object)
Return the identity of the object. This is an integer (or long integer) which is guaranteed to be unique and constant for this object during its lifetime. Two objects with non-overlapping lifetimes may have the same id() value.

```
>>> a=5
>>> id(a)
3885104
>>> b='hello'
>>> id(b)
44148000
```

input([prompt])
This function is used to take input from user and evaluates the expression. There is also raw_input() function which takes input from user, convert it to a string, and returns that.

```
>>> aa=4
>>> bb=6
>>> result1=input('--->')
--->aa+bb
>>> result2=raw_input('--->')
--->aa+bb
>>>
>>> result1
10
>>> result2
'aa+bb'
```

isinstance(object,classinfo)

Return True, if the `object` argument is an instance of the `classinfo` argument, or of a subclass thereof.

```
>>> class new_cls:
...     def __init__(self,x):
...         self.x=x
...
>>> tt=new_cls(10)
>>> isinstance(tt,new_cls)
True
```

Also return `True`, if `classinfo` is a `type` object, and `object` is an object of that `type` or of a subclass thereof. If `object` is not a class instance or an object of the given type, the function always returns `False`.

```
>>> i=5
>>> type(i)
<type 'int'>
>>> type(int)
<type 'type'>
>>> isinstance(i,int)
True
>>> isinstance(i,str)
False
```

If `classinfo` is neither a class object nor a type object, it may be a tuple of class or type objects (other sequence types are not accepted). If `classinfo` is not a class, type, or tuple of classes, types, a `TypeError` exception is raised.

```
>>> isinstance(i,(str,int,float,complex))
True
```

`issubclass(class,classinfo)`
Return `True`, if `class` is a subclass of `classinfo`.

```
>>> class A:
...     pass
...
>>> class B(A):
...     pass
...
>>> class C:
...     pass
...
>>> class D:
...     pass
...
>>> issubclass(B,A)
```

```
True
```

A class is considered a subclass of itself.

```
>>> issubclass(D,D)
True
```

The `classinfo` may be a tuple of class objects, in which case every entry in `classinfo` will be checked. In any other case, a `TypeError` exception is raised.

```
>>> issubclass(B,(A,C,D))
True
```

`len(s)`
Return the length (the number of items) of an object `s`. The argument may be a sequence (string, tuple or list) or a mapping (dictionary).

```
>>> len('abcd')
4
>>> seq=['a','b','c','d']
>>> len(seq)
4
>>> seq=('a','b','c','d')
>>> len(seq)
4
>>> dict={'a':8,'b':9,'c':10,'d':11}
>>> len(dict)
4
>>> len('')
0
```

`locals()`
The function returns a dictionary representing the current local symbol table.

```
#! /usr/bin/env python
# Filemame: LocalScope.py
var1=10
var2=20
def func():
    var3=30
    var4=40
    print 'Local variables of func()=',locals()
func()
if 'var1' in locals().keys() and 'var2' in locals().keys():
    print "'var1' and 'var2' are local variables of this module"
```

Output is:

```
Local variables of func()= {'var4': 40, 'var3': 30}
'var1' and 'var2' are local variables of this module
```

`map(function,iterable, ...)`

Apply `function` to every item of `iterable` and return a list of the results. If additional `iterable` arguments are passed, `function` must take that many arguments and is applied to the items from all iterables in parallel. If one iterable is shorter than another, it is assumed to be extended with `None` items. If function is `None`, the identity function is assumed; if there are multiple arguments, `map()` returns a list consisting of tuples containing the corresponding items from all iterables. The iterable arguments may be a sequence or any iterable object; the result is always a list.

```
>>> def add100(x):
...      return x+100
...
>>> map(add100,(44,22,66))
[144, 122, 166]
>>>
>>> def abc(a,b,c):
...      return a*10000+b*100+c
...
>>> map(abc,(1,2,3),(4,5,6),(7,8,9))
[10407, 20508, 30609]
>>>
>>> map(None,range(3))
[0, 1, 2]
>>> map(None,range(3),'abc',[44, 55, 66])
[(0, 'a', 44), (1, 'b', 55), (2, 'c', 66)]
```

`max(iterable[,key])`

Return the largest item in an `iterable`. The optional argument `key` specifies a function of one argument that is used to extract a comparison key from each list element. The default value is `None` (compare the elements directly).

```
>>> max('hello')
'o'
>>> max([10,80,90,20,-100])
90
>>> def LessThanFifty(x):
...      if x<=50:
...           return x
...
>>> max([10,80,90,20,-100],key=LessThanFifty)
20
```

The function has an another form `max(arg1,arg2,*args[,key])`, which return the largest of two or more arguments.

```
>>> max('hi','hello','bye')
```

```
'hi'
>>> max('Gumby','Lambert','Sartre','cheddar')
'cheddar'
>>> max('Gumby','Lambert','Sartre','cheddar',key=str.upper)
'Sartre'
```

min(iterable[,key])
Return the smallest item in an iterable. The key has same meaning as that in max() function.

```
>>> min('hello')
'e'
>>> min((10,80,90,20,-100))
-100
```

The function has an another form min(arg1,arg2,*args[,key]), which return the smallest of two or more arguments.

```
>>> min(10,80,90,20,-100)
-100
>>> def rev(x): return -x
...
>>> min(10,80,90,20,-100,key=rev)
90
```

next(iterator[,default])
Retrieve the next item from the iterator. If default is given, it is returned if the iterator is exhausted, otherwise StopIteration is raised.

```
>>> it=iter(xrange(0,3))
>>> next(it,'Done')
0
>>> next(it,'Done')
1
>>> next(it,'Done')
2
>>> next(it,'Done')
'Done'
>>> next(it,'Done')
'Done'
>>> it=iter(xrange(0,3))
>>> next(it)
0
>>> next(it)
1
>>> next(it)
2
>>> next(it)
Traceback (most recent call last):
  File "<stdin>", line 1, in <module>
```

```
StopIteration
```

```
oct(x)
```
Convert an integer number (of any size) to an octal string.

```
>>> oct(135)
'0207'
```

```
pow(x,y[,z])
```
Return `x` to the power `y`; if `z` is present, return `x` to the power `y`, and modulo `z` (computed more efficiently than `pow(x,y)%z`). The two-argument form `pow(x,y)` is equivalent to using the power operator `x**y`. The arguments must be of numeric types. If the second argument is negative, the third argument must be omitted. If `z` is present, `x` and `y` must be of integer types, and `y` must be non-negative.

```
>>> 2**4
16
>>> pow(2,4)
16
>>> (2**4)%3
1
>>> pow(2,4,3)
1
```

```
print(*objects,sep=' ',end='\n',file=sys.stdout)
```
Print objects to the stream `file`, separated by `sep` and followed by `end`. If `sep`, `end` and `file`, are present, they must be given as keyword arguments. All non-keyword arguments are converted to strings and written to the stream, separated by `sep` and followed by `end`. Both `sep` and `end` must be strings, they can also be `None`, which means to use the default values. If no `objects` are given, `print()` will just write `end`. The file argument must be an object with a `write()` method, if it is not present or `None`, `sys.stdout` (file objects corresponding to the interpreter's standard output stream) will be used.

This function is not normally available as a built-in function, since the name `print` is recognized as the `print` statement. To disable the statement and use the `print()` function, use the following future statement before using the function.

```
>>> from __future__ import print_function
>>> x,y=3,5
>>> print('The sum of',x,'plus',y,'is',x+y)
The sum of 3 plus 5 is 8
>>> print('The sum of',x,'plus',y,'is',x+y,sep='    ')
The sum of    3    plus    5    is    8
>>> print('The sum of',x,'plus',y,'is',x+y,sep='    ',end='\n The \n
End \n')
The sum of    3    plus    5    is    8
 The
 End
```

```
range(start,stop[,step])
```
This function creates list whose elements are in arithmetic progression. The arguments must be plain integers. If the `step` argument is omitted, it defaults to 1. If the `start` argument is omitted, it defaults to 0. `step` must not be zero (or else `ValueError` is raised).

```
>>> range(10)
[0, 1, 2, 3, 4, 5, 6, 7, 8, 9]
>>> range(1,11)
[1, 2, 3, 4, 5, 6, 7, 8, 9, 10]
>>> range(0,30,5)
[0, 5, 10, 15, 20, 25]
>>> range(0,10,3)
[0, 3, 6, 9]
>>> range(0,-10,-1)
[0, -1, -2, -3, -4, -5, -6, -7, -8, -9]
>>> range(0)
[]
>>> range(10,5)
[]
>>> range(10,5,-1)
[10, 9, 8, 7, 6]
```

```
reload(module)
```
Reload a previously imported `module`. The argument must be a module object, so it must have been successfully imported before. This is useful if the programmer has edited the module's source file using an external editor and wants to try out the new version without leaving the Python interpreter. The return value is the module object.

```
reversed(seq)
```
The function returns an iterator object that can iterate over all the objects in the container in reverse order.

```
>>> Seq=[10,20,30]
>>> revSeq=reversed(Seq)
>>> for item in revSeq: print item
...
30
20
10
```

```
round(number[,ndigits])
```
Return the floating point value `number` rounded to `ndigits` digits after the decimal point. If `ndigits` is omitted, it defaults to zero.

```
>>> round(2.769753)
3.0
>>> round(-2.769753)
```

```
-3.0
>>> round(2.769753,4)
2.7698
>>> round(-2.769753,4)
-2.7698
```

setattr(object,name,value)

This is the counterpart of getattr(). The arguments are an object, a string and an arbitrary value. The string may name an existing attribute or a new attribute. The function assigns the value to the attribute, provided the object allows it. The following example will become clearer after going through chapter 6.

```
>>> class new_cls:
...      def __init__(self,x):
...          self.x=x
...
>>> tt=new_cls(10)
>>> tt.x
10
>>> setattr(tt,'x',20)
>>> tt.x
20
>>> setattr(tt,'y','hello')
>>> tt.y
'hello'
```

slice(start,stop[,step])

Return a slice object representing the set of indices specified by range(start,stop,step). The function can also be of of form slice(stop), where start and step arguments default to None. Slice objects have read-only data attributes start, stop and step, which merely return the argument values (or their default).

```
>>> slice(20)
slice(None, 20, None)
>>> sl=slice(2,20,3)
>>> type(sl)
<type 'slice'>
>>> sl.start
2
>>> sl.stop
20
>>> sl.step
3
```

The slice object can be passed to the __getitem__() method of the built-in sequences.

```
>>> range(50).__getitem__(sl)
[2, 5, 8, 11, 14, 17]
```

[88]

Or use slice objects directly in subscripts:

```
>>> range(50)[sl]
[2, 5, 8, 11, 14, 17]
```

```
sorted(iterable[,cmp[,key[,reverse]]])
```
Return a new sorted list from the items in `iterable`. The arguments `cmp`, `key`, and `reverse` are optional.

```
>>> a=[66.25,333,'abc',333,1,'ab',1234.5]
>>> sorted(a)
[1, 66.25, 333, 333, 1234.5, 'ab', 'abc']
>>> sorted({10:'D',5:'B',8:'B',6:'E',2:'A'})
[2, 5, 6, 8, 10]
```

`cmp` specifies a custom comparison function of two arguments (iterable elements) which should return a negative, zero or positive number depending on whether the first argument is considered smaller than, equal to, or larger than the second argument. The default value is `None`.

`key` specifies a function of one argument that is used to extract a comparison key from each list element. The default value is `None` (compare the elements directly).

```
>>> strs=['ccc','aaaa','d','bb']
>>> sorted(strs,key=len)        # Sorted by string length
['d', 'bb', 'ccc', 'aaaa']
>>> student_tuples=[
... ('john','A',15),
... ('jane','B',12),
... ('dave','B',10),]
>>> sorted(student_tuples,key=lambda student: student[2])   #By age
[('dave', 'B', 10), ('jane', 'B', 12), ('john', 'A', 15)]
```

`reverse` is a boolean value. If set to `True`, then the list elements are sorted as if each comparison were reversed.

```
>>> a=[66.25,333,'abc',333,1,'ab',1234.5]
>>> sorted(a,reverse=True)
['abc', 'ab', 1234.5, 333, 333, 66.25, 1]
```

In general, the `key` and `reverse` conversion processes are much faster than specifying an equivalent `cmp` function. This is because `cmp` is called multiple times for each list element, while `key` and `reverse` touch each element only once.

```
>>> L=['geas','clue','Zoe','Ann']
>>> sorted(L)
['Ann', 'Zoe', 'clue', 'geas']
>>> def ignoreCase(x,y):
```

```
...        return cmp(x.upper(),y.upper())
...
>>> sorted(L,ignoreCase)
['Ann', 'clue', 'geas', 'Zoe']
>>> sorted(L,None,str.upper)
['Ann', 'clue', 'geas', 'Zoe']
>>> L
['geas', 'clue', 'Zoe', 'Ann']
```

sum(iterable[,start])
The function returns the sum total of start (defaults to 0) and the items of an iterable.

```
>>> seq=[5,7.4,2,11]
>>> sum(seq)
25.4
>>> sum(seq,10.2)
35.6
>>> aa=4
>>> bb=2.5
>>> cc=9.1
>>> seq=[aa,bb,cc]
>>> sum(seq)
15.6
```

type(object)
The function returns the type of an object.

```
>>> i=50.7
>>> type(i)
<type 'float'>
>>> type(i) is float
True
```

xrange(start,stop[,step])
This function is very similar to range(), but returns an xrange object instead of a list. This yields the same values as the corresponding list, without actually storing them all simultaneously. The advantage of xrange() over range() is minimal, except when a very large range is used on a memory-starved machine or when all of the range() elements are never used (such as when the loop is usually terminated with break). The function can also be used as xrange(stop).

The xrange type is an immutable sequence which is commonly used for looping. The advantage of the xrange type is that an xrange object will always take the same amount of memory, no matter the size of the range it represents. There are no consistent performance advantages. The xrange objects supports indexing, iteration, and the len() function.

```
>>> for i in xrange(2000000000):
...        print i
...        if i>5:
```

```
...             break
...
0
1
2
3
4
5
6
>>> for i in range(2000000000):
...       print i
...       if i>5:
...             break
...
Traceback (most recent call last):
  File "<stdin>", line 1, in <module>
MemoryError
```

```
zip([iterable, ...])
```
This function returns a list of tuples, where the ith tuple contains the ith element from each of the argument sequences or iterables. The returned list is truncated in length to the length of the shortest argument sequence. When there are multiple arguments which are all of the same length, `zip()` is similar to `map()` with an initial argument of `None`. With no arguments, it returns an empty list. `zip()` in conjunction with the * operator can be used to unzip a list:

```
>>> x=[1,2,3]
>>> y=[4,5,6,7,8]
>>> zipped=zip(x,y)
>>> zipped
[(1, 4), (2, 5), (3, 6)]
>>> zip(x)
[(1,), (2,), (3,)]
>>> x2,y2=zip(*zipped)
>>> x2
(1, 2, 3)
>>> y2
(4, 5, 6)
>>> zip()
[]
```

3.2.5. Scope

A scope defines the visibility of a name within a block. If a local variable is defined in a block, its scope includes that block. If the definition occurs in a function block, the scope extends to any blocks contained within the defining one. The scope of names defined in a class block is limited to the class block. If a name is bound in a block, it is a local variable of that block. If a name is bound at the module level, it is a global variable. The variables of the module code block are local and global.

In Python, variables that are only referenced inside a function are implicitly global. If a variable is ever assigned a new value inside the function, the variable is implicitly local, and the programmer need to explicitly declare it as global.

The scope is bit difficult to understand, the following examples might prove fruitful.

```
def f():
    print s

s="I hate spam"
f()
```

The variable s is defined as the string "I hate spam", before the function call f(). The only statement in f() is the print statement. As there is no local variable s in f(), the value from the global s will be used. So the output will be the string "I hate spam". The question is, what will happen, if the programmer changes the value of s inside of the function f()? Will it affect the global s as well? The test is in the following piece of code:

```
def f():
    s="Me too."
    print s

s="I hate spam."
f()
print s
```

The output looks like the following. It can be observed that s in f() is local variable of f().

```
Me too.
I hate spam.
```

The following example tries to combine the previous two examples i.e. first access s and then assigning a value to it in function f().

```
def f():
    print s
    s="Me too."
    print s

s="I hate spam."
f()
print s
```

The code will raise an exception- UnboundLocalError: local variable 's' referenced before assignment

Python assumes that a local variable is required due to the assignment to s anywhere inside f(), so the first print statement gives the error message. Any variable which is changed or created inside of a function is local, if it has not been declared as a global variable. To tell Python to recognize the variable as global, use the keyword global, as shown in the following example.

```
def f():
    global s
    print s
    s="That's clear."
    print s

s="Python is great!"
f()
print s
```

Now there is no ambiguity. The output is as follows:

```
Python is great!
That's clear.
That's clear.
```

Local variables of functions cannot be accessed from outside the function code block.

```
def f():
    s="I am globally not known"
    print s

f()
print s
```

Executing the above code will give following error message- NameError: name 's' is not defined

3.2.6. Exceptions

Exception is a way of breaking out of the normal flow of control of a code block in order to handle error or other exceptional condition. An exception is raised at the point where the error is detected.

```
>>> while True print 'Hello world'
SyntaxError: invalid syntax
>>> 10/0

Traceback (most recent call last):
  File "<pyshell#1>", line 1, in <module>
    10/0
ZeroDivisionError: integer division or modulo by zero
>>> 4+tt*3

Traceback (most recent call last):
```

```
  File "<pyshell#2>", line 1, in <module>
    4+tt*3
NameError: name 'tt' is not defined
>>> '5'+7

Traceback (most recent call last):
  File "<pyshell#3>", line 1, in <module>
    '5'+7
TypeError: cannot concatenate 'str' and 'int' objects
```

The last line of the error message indicates what went wrong. Exceptions are of different types, and the type is printed as part of the message; the types in the above example are `SyntaxError`, `ZeroDivisionError`, `NameError` and `TypeError`. Standard exception names are built-in identifiers (not reserved keywords). The rest of the lines provides detail based on the type of exception and what caused it.

3.2.6.1. Handling exceptions

If there is some suspicious code that may raise an exception, it can be handled by placing the suspicious code in a `try` compound statement. After the `try` clause, include an `except` clause, followed by a block of code which handles the problem. The following example attempts to open a file and write something in the file.

```
#!/usr/bin/python
try:
   fh = open("testfile", "w")
   fh.write("This is my test file for exception handling!!")
except IOError:
   print "Error: can\'t find file or read data"
else:
   print "Written content in the file successfully"
   fh.close()
```

Here are few important points that needs to be remembered:
- A single `try` statement can have multiple `except` clauses. This is useful when the `try` clause contains statements that may throw different types of exceptions.
- A generic `except` clause can be provided, which handles any exception.
- After the `except` clause(s), an `else` clause can be incuded. The code in the `else` clause is executed, if the code in the `try` clause does not raise an exception.

Chapter 4
DATA STRUCTURES

A data structure is a group of data elements grouped together under one name. Python's data structures are very intuitive from syntax point of view, and they offer a large choice of operations. This chapter tries to put together the most common and useful information about various data structures. Some of the Python's data structures that are discussed in this book are list, tuple, set, and dictionary.

4.1. List
Python has a number of built-in types to group together data items. The most versatile is the list, which is a group of comma-separated values (items) between square brackets. List items need not to be of same data type.

```
>>> a=['spam','eggs',100,1234]
>>> a
['spam', 'eggs', 100, 1234]
```

Python allows adding a trailing comma after last item of list, tuple, and dictionary, . There are several reasons to allow this:
- When the list, tuple, or dictionary elements spread across multiple lines, one needs to remember to add a comma to the previous line. Accidentally omitting the comma can lead to error that might be hard to diagnose. Always adding the comma avoids this source of error (example is given below).
- If comma is placed in each line, they can be reordered without creating a syntax error.

The following example shows the consequence of missing a comma while creating list.

```
>>> a=[
    'hi',
    'hello'
    'bye',
    'tata',
    ]
>>> a
['hi', 'hellobye', 'tata']
```

This list looks like it has four elements, but it actually contains three: `'hi'`, `'hellobye'` and `'tata'`. Always adding the comma avoids this source of error.

4.1.1. List creation
List can be created in many ways.

4.1.1.1. Using square brackets

As discussed before, most common way of creating a list is by enclosing comma-separated values (items) between square brackets. Simply assigning square bracket to a variable creates an empty list.

```
>>> a=[]
>>> a
[]
>>> type(a)
<type 'list'>
```

4.1.1.2. Using other lists

A list can also be created by copying a list or slicing a list.

```
>>> a=['spam','eggs',100,1234]
>>> b=a[:]
>>> b
['spam', 'eggs', 100, 1234]
>>> c=a[1:3]
>>> c
['eggs', 100]
```

4.1.1.3. List comprehension

List comprehension provides a concise way to create list. A list comprehension consist of brackets containing an expression followed by a `for` clause, then zero or more `for` or `if` clauses. The result will be a new list resulting from evaluating the expression in the context of the `for` and `if` clauses which follow it. Common applications are to make new lists where each element is the result of some operations applied to each member of another sequence or iterable, or to create a sub-sequence of those elements that satisfy a certain condition. For example, creating a list of squares using an elaborate approach is as follows:

```
>>> squares=[]
>>> for x in range(10):
...        squares.append(x**2)
...
>>> squares
[0, 1, 4, 9, 16, 25, 36, 49, 64, 81]
```

The same can be obtained using list comprehension as:

```
squares=[x**2 for x in range(10)]
>>> squares
[0, 1, 4, 9, 16, 25, 36, 49, 64, 81]
```

Alternatively, it can also be obtained using `map()` built-in function:

```
squares=map(lambda x: x**2,range(10))
>>> squares
```

```
[0, 1, 4, 9, 16, 25, 36, 49, 64, 81]
```

The following list comprehension combines the elements of two lists if they are not equal:

```
>>> [(x, y) for x in [1,2,3] for y in [3,1,4] if x!=y]
[(1, 3), (1, 4), (2, 3), (2, 1), (2, 4), (3, 1), (3, 4)]
```

and it's equivalent to:

```
>>> combs=[]
>>> for x in [1,2,3]:
...      for y in [3,1,4]:
...          if x!=y:
...              combs.append((x,y))
...
>>> combs
[(1, 3), (1, 4), (2, 3), (2, 1), (2, 4), (3, 1), (3, 4)]
```

4.1.1.4. Using built-in function

List can also be created using built-in function `list()`. The `list([iterable])` function return a list whose items are the same and in the same order as `iterable` items. The `iterable` can be either a sequence, a container that supports iteration, or an iterator object. If iterable is already a list, a copy is made and returned. If no argument is given, a new empty list is returned.

```
>>> list(('hi','hello','bye'))
['hi', 'hello', 'bye']
>>> list('hello')
['h', 'e', 'l', 'l', 'o']
>>> list((10,50,))
[10, 50]
>>> list()
[]
```

4.1.2. Accessing list elements

Like string indices, list indices start at 0. To access values in list, use the square brackets with the index or indices to obtain a slice of the list.

```
>>> a=['spam','eggs',100,1234]
>>> a[0]
'spam'
>>> a[0][1]
'p'
>>> a[1:3]
['eggs', 100]
```

4.1.3. Updating list elements

It is possible to change individual or multiple elements of a list:

```
>>> a=['spam','eggs',100,1234]
>>> a[0]='filter'
>>> a
['filter', 'eggs', 100, 1234]
>>> a[2:4]=455,56858
>>> a
['filter', 'eggs', 455, 56858]
```

The items of list can be updated by the elements of another iterable (list, tuple).

```
>>> a=[66.25,333,333,1,1234.5]
>>> b=['hi','bye']
>>> a[2:4]=b
>>> a
[66.25, 333, 'hi', 'bye', 1234.5]
>>> a=[66.25,333,333,1,1234.5]
>>> b=('hi','bye')
>>> a[2:4]=b
>>> a
[66.25, 333, 'hi', 'bye', 1234.5]
>>> a=[66.25,333,333,1,1234.5]
>>> b=['hi','bye']
>>> a[1:4:2]=b
>>> a
[66.25, 'hi', 333, 'bye', 1234.5]
```

It is also possible to insert elements in a list.

```
>>> a=['spam','eggs',100,1234]
>>> a[1:1]=['chair']
>>> a
['spam', 'chair', 'eggs', 100, 1234]
>>> a[1:1]=['hello','bye']
>>> a
['spam', 'hello', 'bye', 'chair', 'eggs', 100, 1234]
```

To insert a copy of list at the beginning of itself:

```
>>> a=['spam','eggs',100,1234]
>>> a[:0]=a
>>> a
['spam', 'eggs', 100, 1234, 'spam', 'eggs', 100, 1234]
```

There are various methods of list object for updating list, which are discussed in section 4.1.9.

4.1.4. Deleting list elements

To remove a list element, one can use either the `del` statement (if you know the element index to delete) or `remove()` method (if you do not know the element index, but the element itself, discussed in section 4.1.9). The following example depicts deletion of an element using `del` statement.

```
>>> a=['spam','eggs',100,1234]
>>> del a[1]
>>> a
['spam', 100, 1234]
```

The `del` statement can also be used to explicitly remove the entire list.

```
>>> a=['spam','eggs',100,1234]
>>> del a
>>> a
Traceback (most recent call last):
  File "<stdin>", line 1, in <module>
NameError: name 'a' is not defined
```

The following is an interesting case of `del` statement:

```
>>> a=['spam','eggs',100,1234]
>>> del a[1],a[1]
>>> a
['spam', 1234]
```

It should be noted that the same index is deleted twice. As soon as an element is deleted, the indices of succeeding elements are changed. So deleting an index element *n* times, would actually delete *n* elements.

It is also possible to delete multiple items of a list.

```
>>> a=['spam','eggs',100,1234]
>>> a[1:3]=[]
>>> a
['spam', 1234]
```

4.1.5. Swapping lists

There might be a scenario in which multiple lists needs to be swapped among themselves. This is can done easily using multiple assignments expression.

```
>>> a=[10,20,30]
>>> b=[40,50,60]
>>> c=[70,80,90]
>>> a,b,c=c,a,b
>>> a
[70, 80, 90]
```

```
>>> b
[10, 20, 30]
>>> c
[40, 50, 60]
```

4.1.6. Looping techniques

List can also be used in iteration operation, for example:

```
>>> for a in [4,6,9,2]: print a
...
4
6
9
2
>>> for a in [4,6,9,2]: print a,
...
4 6 9 2
```

When looping through a sequence, the position index and corresponding value can be retrieved at the same time using the enumerate() function.

```
>>> for i,v in enumerate(['tic','tac','toe']):
...     print i,v
...
0 tic
1 tac
2 toe
```

To loop over two or more sequences at the same time, the entries can be paired with the zip() function.

```
>>> questions=['name','quest','favorite color']
>>> answers=['lancelot','the holy grail','blue']
>>> for q,a in zip(questions,answers):
...     print 'What is your {0}?  It is {1}.'.format(q,a)
...
What is your name?  It is lancelot.
What is your quest?  It is the holy grail.
What is your favorite color?  It is blue.
```

While iterating a mutable sequence, if there is a need to change the sequence (for example to duplicate certain items), it is recommended to make a copy of the sequence before starting iteration. Looping over a sequence does not implicitly make a copy. The slice notation makes this especially convenient.

```
>>> words=['cat','window','defenestrate']
>>> for w in words[:]:
...     if len(w)>6:
```

```
...           words.insert(0,w)
...
>>> words
['defenestrate', 'cat', 'window', 'defenestrate']
```

4.1.7.   Nested list

It is possible to nest lists (create list containing other lists), for example:

```
>>> q=[2,3]
>>> p=[1,q,4]
>>> len(p)
3
>>> p[1]
[2, 3]
>>> p[1][0]
2
>>> p[1].append('xtra')
>>> p
[1, [2, 3, 'xtra'], 4]
>>> q
[2, 3, 'xtra']
```

Note that in the last example, p[1] and q refer to the same object, which can cross-checked using id() built-in function.

```
>>> id(q)
104386192
>>> id(p[1])
104386192
```

4.1.8.   Some list operations

Some of the list operations supported by Python are given below.

4.1.8.1.   Concatenation

List concatenation can be carried out using + operator.

```
>>> [1,2,3]+['hi','hello']
[1, 2, 3, 'hi', 'hello']
```

4.1.8.2.   Repetition

The * operator can be used to carry out repetition operation.

```
>>> ['Hey']*3
['Hey', 'Hey', 'Hey']
```

4.1.8.3.   Membership operation

List also supports membership operation i.e. checking the existence of an element in a list.

```
>>> 4 in [6,8,1,3,5,0]
False
>>> 1 in [6,8,1,3,5,0]
True
```

4.1.8.4. Slicing operation

As list is a sequence, so indexing and slicing work the same way for list as they do for strings. All slice operations return a new list containing the requested elements:

```
>>> a=['spam','eggs',100,1234]
>>> a[2]
100
>>> a[-2]
100
>>> a[1:3]
['eggs', 100]
>>> a[:]
['spam', 'eggs', 100, 1234]
```

List slicing can be in form of steps, the operation `s[i:j:k]` slices the list `s` from `i` to `j` with step `k`.

```
>>> squares=[x**2 for x in range(10)]
>>> squares
[0, 1, 4, 9, 16, 25, 36, 49, 64, 81, 100, 121, 144, 169, 196]
>>> squares[2:12:3]
[4, 25, 64, 121]
```

Slice indices have useful defaults, an omitted first index defaults to zero, an omitted second index defaults to the size of the list being sliced.

```
>>> squares=[x**2 for x in range(10)]
>>> squares
[0, 1, 4, 9, 16, 25, 36, 49, 64, 81, 100, 121, 144, 169, 196]
>>> squares[5:]
[25, 36, 49, 64, 81, 100, 121, 144, 169, 196]
>>> squares[:5]
[0, 1, 4, 9, 16]
```

4.1.9. List methods

Below are the methods of list objects.

`list.append(x)`
Add an item to the end of the list. It is same as `list[len(list):len(list)]=[x]`.

```
>>> a=[66.25,333,333,1,1234.5]
>>> a.append(45)
>>> a
```

```
[66.25, 333, 333, 1, 1234.5, 45]
>>> a=[66.25,333,333,1,1234.5]
>>> a[len(a):len(a)]=[45]
>>> a
[66.25, 333, 333, 1, 1234.5, 45]
```

`list.extend(L)`

Extend a list by appending all the items of a given list. It is same as `list[len(list): len(list)]=L`.

```
>>> a=[66.25,333,333,1,1234.5]
>>> b=[7.3,6.8]
>>> a.extend(b)
>>> a
[66.25, 333, 333, 1, 1234.5, 7.3, 6.8]
>>> a=[66.25,333,333,1,1234.5]
>>> b=[7.3,6.8]
>>> a[len(a):len(a)]=b
>>> a
[66.25, 333, 333, 1, 1234.5, 7.3, 6.8]
```

`list.insert(i,x)`

Insert an item at a given position in the list. The first argument i is the index before which an item x need to be inserted. It is same as `list[i:i]=[x]`.

```
>>> a=[66.25,333,333,1,1234.5]
>>> a.insert(2,5.7)
>>> a
[66.25, 333, 5.7, 333, 1, 1234.5]
>>> a=[66.25,333,333,1,1234.5]
>>> a[2:2]=[5.7]
>>> a
[66.25, 333, 5.7, 333, 1, 1234.5]
```

`list.index(x[,i[,j]])`

Return the index in the list of the first occurrence of item x. In other words, it returns the smallest index k such that `list[k]==x` and `i<=k<j`. A `ValueError` exception is raised in absence of item x.

```
>>> a=[66.25,333,333,1,1234.5]
>>> a.index(333)
1
```

`list.remove(x)`

Remove the first item from the list whose value is x. An error (`ValueError` exception) occur in absence of item x. It is same as `del list[list.index(x)]`.

```
>>> a=[66.25,333,333,1,1234.5]
```

```
>>> a.remove(333)
>>> a
[66.25, 333, 1, 1234.5]
>>> a=[66.25,333,333,1,1234.5]
>>> del a[a.index(333)]
>>> a
[66.25, 333, 1, 1234.5]
```

`list.pop([i])`
Remove the item at the given position i in the list, and return it. If no index is specified (defaults to -1), `pop()` removes and returns the last item in the list.

```
>>> a=[66.25,333,333,1,1234.5]
>>> a.pop(3)
1
>>> a
[66.25, 333, 333, 1234.5]
>>> a.pop()
1234.5
>>> a
[66.25, 333, 333]
```

`list.count(x)`
Return the number of times item x appears in the list.

```
>>> a=[66.25,333,333,1,1234.5]
>>> a.count(333)
2
```

`list.reverse()`
Reverse the element's position in the list; no new list is returned. It is same as `list=list[::-1]`.

```
>>> a=[66.25,333,333,1,1234.5]
>>> a.reverse()
>>> a
[1234.5, 1, 333, 333, 66.25]
>>> a=[66.25,333,333,1,1234.5]
>>> a=a[::-1]
[1234.5, 1, 333, 333, 66.25]
```

`list.sort([cmp[,key[,reverse]]])`
Sort the items of the list; no new list is returned. The optional arguments have same meaning as given in `sorted()` built-in function.

```
>>> a=[66.25,333,333,1,1234.5]
>>> a.sort()
>>> a
[1, 66.25, 333, 333, 1234.5]
```

```
>>> a=[66.25,333,'abc',333,1,'ab',1234.5]
>>> a.sort()
>>> a
[1, 66.25, 333, 333, 1234.5, 'ab', 'abc']
>>> a=[66.25,333,'abc',333,1,'ab',1234.5]
>>> a.sort(reverse=True)
>>> a
['abc', 'ab', 1234.5, 333, 333, 66.25, 1]
```

4.1.10. Using list as Stack

The list methods make it very easy to use a list as a stack, where the last element added is the first element retrieved ("last-in, first-out" approach). To add an item to the top of the stack, use `append()`. To retrieve an item from the top of the stack, use `pop()` without an explicit index. For example:

```
>>> stack=[3,4,5]
>>> stack.append(6)
>>> stack.append(7)
>>> stack
[3, 4, 5, 6, 7]
>>> stack.pop()
7
>>> stack
[3, 4, 5, 6]
>>> stack.pop()
6
>>> stack.pop()
5
>>> stack
[3, 4]
```

4.1.11. Using list as queue

It is also possible to use a list as a queue, where the first element added is the first element retrieved ("first-in, first-out"); however, list is not efficient for this purpose. While appending and popping of elements from the end of list are fast, doing inserting and popping from the beginning of a list is slow (because all of the other elements have to be shifted by one).

To implement a queue, use `collections.deque` which was designed to have fast appends and pops from both ends. For example:

```
>>> from collections import deque
>>> queue=deque(["Eric","John","Michael"])
>>> queue.append("Terry")
>>> queue.append("Graham")
>>> queue
deque(['Eric', 'John', 'Michael', 'Terry', 'Graham'])
>>> queue.popleft()
'Eric'
```

```
>>> queue.popleft()
'John'
>>> queue
deque(['Michael', 'Terry', 'Graham'])
```

4.2. Tuple

There is also another sequence type- tuple. Tuples is a sequence just like list. The differences are that tuple cannot be changed i.e. tuple is immutable, while list is mutable, and tuple use parentheses, while list use square brackets. Tuple items need not to be of same data type. Also, as mentioned previously, Python allow adding a trailing comma after last item of tuple.

```
>>> a=('spam','eggs',100,1234)
>>> a
('spam', 'eggs', 100, 1234)
>>> a=('spam','eggs',100,1234,)
>>> a
('spam', 'eggs', 100, 1234)
```

The above expressions are examples of "tuple packing" operation i.e. the values `'spam'`, `'eggs'`, `100` and `1234` are packed together in a tuple. The reverse operation is also possible, for example:

```
>>> a1,a2,a3,a4=a
>>> a1
'spam'
>>> a2
'eggs'
>>> a3
100
>>> a4
1234
```

This is called "sequence unpacking", and works for any sequence on the right-hand side. Sequence unpacking requires the group of variables on the left to have the same number of elements as the length of the sequence. Note that multiple assignments are really just a combination of tuple packing and sequence unpacking.

```
>>> a,b=10,20
>>> a
10
>>> b
20
```

4.2.1. Tuple creation

Tuple can be created in many ways.

4.2.1.1. Using parenthesis

Creating a tuple is as simple as grouping various comma-separated values, and optionally these comma-separated values between parentheses.

```
>>> a=('spam','eggs',100,1234)
>>> a
('spam', 'eggs', 100, 1234)
>>> a=('spam','eggs',100,1234,)
>>> a
('spam', 'eggs', 100, 1234)
>>> a='spam','eggs',100,1234
>>> a
('spam', 'eggs', 100, 1234)
>>> a='spam','eggs',100,1234,
>>> a
('spam', 'eggs', 100, 1234)
```

A tuple with one item is created by a comma after the item (it is not necessary to enclose a single item in parentheses).

```
>>> a=(10)
>>> a
10
>>> type(a)
<type 'int'>
>>> b=(10,)
>>> b
(10,)
>>> type(b)
<type 'tuple'>
>>> c=10,
>>> c
(10,)
>>> type(c)
<type 'tuple'>
```

It is also possible to create an empty tuple by assigning parenthesis to a variable.

```
>>> a=()
>>> a
()
```

4.2.1.2. Using other tuples

A tuple can also be created by copying a tuple or slicing a tuple.

```
>>> a=('spam','eggs',100,1234)
>>> b=a[:]
>>> b
```

```
('spam', 'eggs', 100, 1234)
>>> c=a[1:3]
>>> c
('eggs', 100)
```

4.2.1.3. Using built-in function

Tuple can also be created using built-in function `tuple()`. The `tuple([iterable])` function return a tuple whose items are same and in the same order as items of the `iterable`. The `iterable` may be a sequence, a container that supports iteration, or an iterator object. If `iterable` is already a tuple, it is returned unchanged. If no argument is given, an empty tuple is returned.

```
>>> tuple(['apple','pineapple','banana'])
('apple', 'pineapple', 'banana')
>>> tuple('apple')
('a', 'p', 'p', 'l', 'e')
>>> tuple(['apple'])
('apple',)
```

4.2.2. Accessing tuple elements

The tuple index start with 0, and to access values in tuple, use the square brackets with the index or indices to obtain a slice of the tuple.

```
>>> a=('spam','eggs',100,1234)
>>> a[0]
'spam'
>>> a[1:3]
('eggs', 100)
```

4.2.3. Update tuple

Tuple is immutable, so changing element value or adding new elements is not possible. But one can take portions of existing tuples to create a new tuples.

```
>>> tuple1=(1,2,3)
>>> tuple2=('a','b','c')
>>> tuple3=tuple1+tuple2
>>> tuple3
(1, 2, 3, 'a', 'b', 'c')
>>> tuple3=tuple1[0:2]+tuple2[1:3]
>>> tuple3
(1, 2, 'b', 'c')
```

It is also possible to create tuple which contain mutable objects, such as lists.

```
>>> a=[1,2,3],[4,5,6,7]
>>> a
([1, 2, 3], [4, 5, 6, 7])
```

```
>>> a[0][1]=200
>>> a
([1, 200, 3], [4, 5, 6, 7])
```

4.2.4. Deleting tuple

Removing individual tuple element is not possible. To explicitly remove an entire tuple, just use the `del` statement.

```
>>> a=('spam','eggs',100,1234)
>>> del a
```

4.2.5. Swapping tuples

There might be a scenario in which multiple tuples needs to be swapped among themselves. This is can done easily using multiple assignments expression.

```
>>> a=(10,20,30)
>>> b=(40,50,60)
>>> c=(70,80,90)
>>> a,b,c=c,a,b
>>> a
(70, 80, 90)
>>> b
(10, 20, 30)
>>> c
(40, 50, 60)
```

4.2.6. Looping techniques

Tuple can also be used in iteration operation, for example:

```
>>> for a in (4,6,9,2): print a
...
4
6
9
2
>>> for a in (4,6,9,2): print a,
...
4 6 9 2
```

When looping through a sequence, the position index and corresponding value can be retrieved at the same time using the `enumerate()` function.

```
>>> for i,v in enumerate(('tic','tac','toe')):
...     print i,v
...
0 tic
1 tac
2 toe
```

To loop over two or more sequences at the same time, the entries can be paired with the `zip()` function.

```
>>> questions=('name','quest','favorite color')
>>> answers=('lancelot','the holy grail','blue')
>>> for q,a in zip(questions,answers):
...     print 'What is your {0}?  It is {1}.'.format(q,a)
...
What is your name?  It is lancelot.
What is your quest?  It is the holy grail.
What is your favorite color?  It is blue.
```

4.2.7. Nested tuple
It is possible to create nested tuples.

```
>>> q=(2,3)
>>> r=[5,6]
>>> p=(1,q,4,r)
>>> len(p)
4
>>> p[1]
(2, 3)
>>> p[1][0]
2
>>> p[3]
[5, 6]
>>> p
(1, (2, 3), 4, [5, 6])
```

Note that in the last example, `p[1]` and `q` refer to the same object, also `p[3]` and `r` refer to the same object.

4.2.8. Some tuple operations
Some of the tuple operations supported by Python are given below.

4.2.8.1. Concatenation
Tuple concatenation can be carried out using + operator.

```
>>> (1,2,3)+('hi','hello')
(1, 2, 3, 'hi', 'hello')
```

4.2.8.2. Repetition
The * operator can be used to carry out repetition operation.

```
>>> ('Hey',)*3
('Hey', 'Hey', 'Hey')
```

4.2.8.3. Membership operation

Tuple also supports membership operation i.e. checking the existence of an element in a tuple.

```
>>> 4 in (6,8,1,3,5,0)
False
>>> 1 in (6,8,1,3,5,0)
True
```

4.2.8.4. Slicing operation

As tuple is a sequence, so indexing and slicing work the same way for tuple as they do for strings. All slice operations returns a new tuple containing the requested elements:

```
>>> a=('spam','eggs',100,1234)
>>> a[2]
100
>>> a[-2]
100
>>> a[1:3]
('eggs', 100)
>>> a[:]
('spam', 'eggs', 100, 1234)
```

Tuple slicing can be in form of steps, the operation `s[i:j:k]` slices the tuple `s` from `i` to `j` with step `k`.

```
>>> squares=(0,1,4,9,16,25,36,49,64,81,100,121,144,169,196)
>>> squares[2:12:3]
(4, 25, 64, 121)
```

Slice indices have useful defaults, an omitted first index defaults to zero, an omitted second index defaults to the size of the tuple being sliced.

```
>>> squares=(0,1,4,9,16,25,36,49,64,81,100,121,144,169,196)
>>> squares[5:]
(25, 36, 49, 64, 81, 100, 121, 144, 169, 196)
>>> squares[:5]
(0, 1, 4, 9, 16)
```

4.3. Set

A set is an unordered collection with no duplicate elements. Basic uses include membership testing, eliminating duplicate entries from sequence, mathematical operations like union, intersection, difference, symmetric difference etc. As mentioned in chapter 2, sets are of two types: set (mutable set) and frozenset (immutable set).

```
>>> a=set(['spam','eggs',100,1234])
>>> a
```

```
set(['eggs', 100, 1234, 'spam'])
>>> a=set('abracadabra')
>>> a
set(['a', 'r', 'b', 'c', 'd'])
>>> a=frozenset(['spam','eggs',100,1234])
>>> a
frozenset(['eggs', 100, 1234, 'spam'])
```

Being an unordered collection, sets do not record element position or order of insertion. Accordingly, sets do not support indexing, slicing, or other sequence-like behavior.

4.3.1. Set creation
A set can be created in many ways.

4.3.1.1. Using curly braces
Non-empty set (not frozenset) can be created by placing a comma-separated list of elements within braces. Curly braces cannot be used to create an empty set, because it will create an empty dictionary that will be discussed in the next section.

```
>>> {'spam','eggs',100,1234}
set([1234, 100, 'eggs', 'spam'])
```

4.3.1.2. Set comprehension
Python also supports set comprehension:

```
>>> a={x for x in 'abracadabra' if x not in 'abc'}
>>> a
set(['r', 'd'])
```

4.3.1.3. Using built-in function
The built-in functions set() and frozenset() are used to create set and frozenset, respectively, whose elements are taken from iterable. If iterable is not specified, a new empty set is returned.

```
>>> a=set(('spam','eggs',100,1234))
>>> a
set(['eggs', 100, 1234, 'spam'])
>>> set()
set([])
>>> a=frozenset(('spam','eggs',100,1234))
>>> a
frozenset(['eggs', 100, 1234, 'spam'])
>>> frozenset()
frozenset([])
>>> set('abc')==frozenset('abc')
True
```

4.3.2. Deleting set

To explicitly remove an entire set, just use the `del` statement.

```
>>> ss=set('abracadabra')
>>> ss
set(['a', 'r', 'b', 'c', 'd'])
>>> del ss
>>> ss
Traceback (most recent call last):
  File "<stdin>", line 1, in <module>
NameError: name 'ss' is not defined
```

4.3.3. Looping techniques

It is also possible to iterate over each element of a set. However, since set is unordered, it is not known which order the iteration will follow.

```
>>> ss=set('abracadabra')
>>> ss
set(['a', 'r', 'b', 'c', 'd'])
>>> for item in ss:
...     print item
...
a
r
b
c
d
```

4.3.4. Membership operation

Set also support membership operation.

```
>>> a=set('abracadabra')
>>> a
set(['a', 'r', 'b', 'c', 'd'])
>>> 'r' in a
True
>>> 'rrr' not in a
True
>>> a=frozenset('abracadabra')
>>> a
frozenset(['a', 'r', 'b', 'c', 'd'])
>>> 'r' in a
True
>>> 'rrr' not in a
True
```

4.3.5. Set methods

Below are the methods of both `set` and `frozenset` objects. Note that the non-operator versions of these methods accepts any iterable as an argument, while their operator based counterparts require their arguments to be sets (set and frozenset).

`isdisjoint(other)`

Return `True`, if the set has no elements in common with `other`. Sets are disjoint, if and only if their intersection is the empty set.

```
>>> s1=set([5,10,15,20])
>>> s2=set([30,35,40])
>>> s1.isdisjoint(s2)
True
>>> s1=frozenset([5,10,15,20])
>>> s2=frozenset([30,35,40])
>>> s1.isdisjoint(s2)
True
>>> s1=set([5,10,15,20])
>>> s2=frozenset([30,35,40])
>>> s1.isdisjoint(s2)
True
```

`issubset(other)`

Test whether every element in the set is in `other`.

```
>>> s1=set([5,15])
>>> s2=set([5,10,15,20])
>>> s1.issubset(s2)
True
>>> s1.issubset((5,10,15,20))
True
>>> s1=frozenset([5,15])
>>> s2=frozenset([5,10,15,20])
>>> s1.issubset(s2)
True
>>> s1.issubset((5,10,15,20))
True
```

The operator based version of the the above method is `set<=other`.

```
>>> s1=set([5,15])
>>> s2=frozenset([5,10,15,20])
>>> s1<=s2
True
```

The operator based version `set<other` test whether the `set` is a proper subset of `other`, that is, `set<=other` and `set!=other`.

```
>>> s1=set([5,15])
>>> s2=frozenset([5,10,15,20])
>>> s1<s2
True
```

issuperset(other)
Test whether every element in other is in the set.

```
>>> s1=set([5,15])
>>> s2=set([5,10,15,20])
>>> s2.issuperset(s1)
True
>>> s2.issuperset((5,15))
True
>>> s1=frozenset([5,15])
>>> s2=frozenset([5,10,15,20])
>>> s2.issuperset(s1)
True
>>> s2.issuperset((5,15))
```

The operator based version of the the above method is set>=other.

```
>>> s1=set([5,15])
>>> s2=frozenset([5,10,15,20])
>>> s1>=s2
False
```

The operator based version set>other test whether the set is a proper superset of other, that is, set>=other and set!=other.

```
>>> s1=set([5,15])
>>> s2=frozenset([5,10,15,20])
>>> s1<s2
False
```

union(other, ...)
Return a new set with elements from the set and all others.

```
>>> s1=set([5,15])
>>> s2=[15,20,25]
>>> s3=frozenset([30,35,40])
>>> s1.union(s2,s3)
set([35, 20, 5, 40, 25, 30, 15])
```

The operator based version of the the above method is set|other...

```
>>> s1=set([5,15])
>>> s2=set([15,20,25])
```

```
>>> s3=frozenset([30,35,40])
>>> s1|s2|s3
set([35, 20, 5, 40, 25, 30, 15])
```

```
intersection(other, ...)
```
Return a new set with elements common to the set and all others .

```
>>> s1=set([5,10,15])
>>> s2=[15,20,25,10]
>>> s3=frozenset([30,15,35,40,10])
>>> s4=(40,50,10,15,20)
>>> s1.intersection(s2,s3,s4)
set([10, 15])
```

The operator based version of the the above method is `set&other...`

```
>>> s1=set([5,10,15])
>>> s2=set([15,20,25,10])
>>> s3=frozenset([30,15,35,40,10])
>>> s4=frozenset([40,50,10,15,20])
>>> s1&s2&s3&s4
set([10, 15])
```

```
difference(other, ...)
```
Return a new set with elements in the set that are not in the others.

```
>>> s1=set([5,10,15])
>>> s2=[15,20,25,10]
>>> s3=frozenset([30,15,35,40,10])
>>> s4=(40,50,10,15,20)
>>> s3.difference(s1,s2,s4)
frozenset([35, 30])
```

The operator based version of the the above method is `set-other-...`

```
>>> s1=set([5,10,15])
>>> s2=set([15,20,25,10])
>>> s3=frozenset([30,15,35,40,10])
>>> s4=frozenset([40,50,10,15,20])
>>> s1-s2-s3-s4
set([5])
>>> s3-s1-s2-s4
frozenset([35, 30])
```

```
symmetric_difference(other)
```
Return a new set with elements in either the set or `other` but not both.

```
>>> s1=set([5,10,15])
```

[116]

```
>>> s2=[15,20,25,10]
>>> s1.symmetric_difference(s2)
set([25, 20, 5])
```

The operator based version of the the above method is `set^other`.

```
>>> s1=set([5,10,15])
>>> s2=frozenset([15,20,25,10])
>>> s1^s2
set([25, 20, 5])
>>> s2^s1
frozenset([25, 20, 5])
```

`copy()`
Return a copy of the set.

```
>>> s=set([5,10,15,20])
>>> a=s.copy()
>>> a
set([10, 20, 5, 15])
>>> s=frozenset([5,10,15,20])
>>> a=s.copy()
>>> a
frozenset([10, 20, 5, 15])
```

The following methods are available for `set` and do not apply to immutable instances of `frozenset`.

`update(other, ...)`
Update the set, adding elements from all others.

```
>>> s1=set([5,15])
>>> s2=(15,20,25)
>>> s3=frozenset([30,35,40])
>>> s1.update(s2,s3)
>>> s1
set([35, 20, 5, 40, 25, 30, 15])
```

The operator based version of the the above method is `set|=other|...`

```
>>> s1=set([5,15])
>>> s2=set([15,20,25])
>>> s3=frozenset([30,35,40])
>>> s1|=s2|s3
>>> s1
set([35, 5, 40, 15, 20, 25, 30])
```

`intersection_update(other, ...)`
Update the set, keeping only elements found in it and all others.

```
>>> s1=set([5,10,15])
>>> s2=[15,20,25,10]
>>> s3=set([30,15,35,40,10])
>>> s4=(40,50,10,15,20)
>>> s1.intersection_update(s2,s3,s4)
>>> s1
set([10, 15])
```

The operator based version of the the above method is `set&=other&...`

```
>>> s1=set([5,10,15])
>>> s2=set([15,20,25,10])
>>> s3=frozenset([30,15,35,40,10])
>>> s4=frozenset([40,50,10,15,20])
>>> s1&=s2&s3&s4
>>> s1
set([10, 15])
```

`difference_update(other, ...)`
Update the set, removing elements found in others.

```
>>> s1=frozenset([5,10,15])
>>> s2=[15,20,25,10]
>>> s3=set([30,15,35,40,10])
>>> s4=(40,50,10,15,20)
>>> s3.difference_update(s1,s2,s4)
>>> s3
set([35, 30])
```

The operator based version of the the above method is `set-=other|...`

```
>>> s1=frozenset([5,10,15])
>>> s2=frozenset([15,20,25,10])
>>> s3=set([30,15,35,40,10])
>>> s4=frozenset([40,50,10,15,20])
>>> s3-=s1|s2|s4
>>> s3
set([35, 30])
```

`symmetric_difference_update(other)`
Update the set, keeping only elements found in either set, but not in both.

```
>>> s1=set([5,10,15])
>>> s2=[15,20,25,10]
>>> s1.symmetric_difference_update(s2)
>>> s1
set([25, 20, 5])
```

[118]

The operator based version of the the above method is `set^=other`.

```
>>> s1=set([5,10,15])
>>> s2=frozenset([15,20,25,10])
>>> s1^=s2
>>> s1
set([25, 20, 5])
```

`add(elem)`
The method adds element `elem` to the set.

```
>>> s=set([5,10,15,20])
>>> s.add(25)
>>> s
set([25, 10, 20, 5, 15])
```

`remove(elem)`
Remove element `elem` from the set. Raises `KeyError`, if `elem` is not contained in the set.

```
>>> s=set([5,10,15,20])
>>> s.remove(15)
>>> s
set([10, 20, 5])
>>> s=set([5,10,15,20])
>>> s.remove(100)
Traceback (most recent call last):
  File "<stdin>", line 1, in <module>
KeyError: 100
```

`discard(elem)`
Remove element `elem` from the set if it is present. It is difference from `remove()` in a way that it does not raise `KeyError` if `elem` is not present in the set.

```
>>> s=set([5,10,15,20])
>>> s.discard(15)
>>> s
set([10, 20, 5])
>>> s.discard(100)
>>> s
set([10, 20, 5])
```

`pop()`
Remove and return an arbitrary element from the set. Raises `KeyError`, if the set is empty.

```
>>> s=set([5,10,15,20])
>>> s.pop()
10
>>> s
```

```
set([20, 5, 15])
>>> s.pop()
20
>>> s
set([5, 15])
```

```
clear()
```
Remove all elements from the set.

```
>>> s=set([5,10,15,20])
>>> s.clear()
>>> s
set([])
```

4.4. Dictionary

Another useful mutable built-in type is "dictionary". A dictionary as an unordered group of comma separated "key : value" pairs enclosed within braces, with the requirement that the keys are unique within a dictionary. The main operation on a dictionary is storing a value corresponding to a given key and extracting the value for that given key. Unlike sequences, which are indexed by a range of numbers, dictionary is indexed by key (key should be of immutable type, strings and numbers can always be keys). Tuples can be used as keys if they contain only strings, numbers, or tuples; if a tuple contains any mutable object either directly or indirectly, it cannot be used as a key. List cannot be used as keys, since lists are of mutable type. Also, as mentioned previously, Python allow adding a trailing comma after last item of the dictionary.

```
>>> a={'sape':4139,'guido':4127,'jack':4098}
>>> a
{'sape': 4139, 'jack': 4098, 'guido': 4127}
>>> a['jack']
4098
>>> a={'sape':4139,'guido':4127,'jack':4098,}
>>> a
{'sape': 4139, 'jack': 4098, 'guido': 4127}
```

4.4.1. Dictionary creation

Dictionary can be created in many ways.

4.4.1.1. Using curly braces

Placing a comma-separated record of key-value pairs within the braces adds initial key-value pairs to the dictionary; this is also the way dictionaries are written as output.

```
>>> a={'sape':4139,'guido':4127,'jack':4098}
>>> a
{'sape': 4139, 'jack': 4098, 'guido': 4127}
```

A pair of braces creates an empty dictionary.

```
>>> a={}
>>> a
{}
>>> type(a)
<type 'dict'>
```

4.4.1.2. Dictionary comprehension
Dictionary comprehension provides a concise way to create dictionary.

```
>>> {x: x**2 for x in (2,4,6)}
{2: 4, 4: 16, 6: 36}
```

4.4.1.3. Using built-in function
Dictionary can also be created using built-in function `dict()`. Consider the following example using `dict()`, which returns the same dictionary `{"one":1,"two":2,"three":3}`:

```
>>> a=dict(one=1,two=2,three=3)
>>> b={'one':1,'two':2,'three':3}
>>> c=dict(zip(['one','two','three'],[1,2,3]))
>>> d=dict([('two',2),('one',1),('three',3)])
>>> e=dict({'three':3,'one':1,'two':2})
>>> a==b==c==d==e
True
```

4.4.2. Accessing dictionary elements
To access a dictionary value, use key enclosed within square bracket. A `KeyError` exception is raised if the key is not present in the dictionary.

```
>>> a={'sape':4139,'guido':4127,'jack':4098}
>>> a['guido']
4127
```

4.4.3. Updating dictionary elements
It is possible to add new item in a dictionary and can also change value for a given key.

```
>>> a={'sape':4139,'guido':4127,'jack':4098}
>>> a['mike']=2299         # Add new item
>>> a['guido']=1000        # Update existing item
>>> a
{'sape': 4139, 'mike': 2299, 'jack': 4098, 'guido': 1000}
```

It is also possible to update a dictionary with another dictionary using `update()` method (discussed later).

4.4.4. Deleting dictionary elements
To remove a dictionary item (key-value pair) or the entire dictionary, one can use the `del` statement. To remove all items (resulting an empty dictionary), `clear()` method (discussed later) can be used.

```
>>> a={'sape':4139,'guido':4127,'jack':4098}
>>> del a['guido']
>>> a
{'sape': 4139, 'jack': 4098}
>>> del a
>>> a
Traceback (most recent call last):
  File "<stdin>", line 1, in <module>
NameError: name 'a' is not defined
```

4.4.5. Membership operation

Dictionary support membership operation i.e. checking the existence of a key in the dictinary.

```
>>> a={'sape':4139,'guido':4127,'jack':4098}
>>> 'jack' in a
True
>>> 'tom' not in a
True
>>> 4127 in a
False
```

4.4.6. Looping techniques

When looping through dictionary, the key and corresponding value can be retrieved at the same time using the `iteritems()` method.

```
>>> a={'sape':4139,'guido':4127,'jack':4098}
>>> for k,v in a.iteritems():
...      print k,v
...
sape 4139
jack 4098
guido 4127
```

4.4.7. Dictionary methods

The following are some dictionary methods supported by Python.

`dict.clear()`
Removes all items from the dictionary.

```
>>> a={'Name':'Zara','Age':7}
>>> len(a)
2
>>> a.clear()
>>> len(a)
0
```

`dict.copy()`

Returns a copy of dictionary.

```
>>> dict1={'Name':'Zara','Age':7}
>>> dict2=dict1.copy()
>>> dict2
{'Age': 7, 'Name': 'Zara'}
```

`dict.fromkeys(seq[,value])`
Create a new dictionary with keys from `seq` and values set to `value` (default as `None`).

```
>>> seq=('name','age','gender')
>>> a=dict.fromkeys(seq)
>>> a
{'gender': None, 'age': None, 'name': None}
>>> a=a.fromkeys(seq,10)
>>> a
{'gender': 10, 'age': 10, 'name': 10}
```

`dict.get(key[,default])`
Return the value for `key`, if `key` is in the dictionary, else `default`. If `default` is not given, the default is `None`.

```
>>> a={'Name':'Zara','Age':7}
>>> a.get('Age')
7
>>> a.get('Gender','Never')
'Never'
>>> print a.get('Gender')
None
```

`dict.has_key(key)`
Test for the presence of `key` in the dictionary. Returns `True`, if `key` is present in dictionary, otherwise `False`.

```
>>> a={'Name':'Zara','Age':7}
>>> a.has_key('Age')
True
>>> a.has_key('Gender')
False
```

`dict.items()`
Returns a list of dictionary's key-value tuple pairs.

```
>>> a={'Name':'Zara','Age':7}
>>> a.items()
[('Age', 7), ('Name', 'Zara')]
```

`dict.iteritems()`

Returns an iterator over the dictionary's key-value pairs.

```
>>> a={'Gender':'Female','Age':7,'Hair color':None,'Name':'Zara'}
>>> for b in a.iteritems():
...     print '{0}----{1}'.format(b[0],b[1])
...
Gender----Female
Age----7
Hair color----None
Name----Zara
```

```
dict.iterkeys()
```
Returns an iterator over the dictionary's keys.

```
>>> a={'Gender':'Female','Age':7,'Hair color':None,'Name':'Zara'}
>>> for b in a.iterkeys():
...     print b
...
Gender
Age
Hair color
Name
```

```
dict.itervalues()
```
Returns an iterator over the dictionary's values.

```
>>> a={'Gender':'Female','Age':7,'Hair color':None,'Name':'Zara'}
>>> for b in a.itervalues():
...     print b
...
Female
7
None
Zara
```

```
dict.keys()
```
Returns list of dictionary keys.

```
>>> a={'Name':'Zara','Age':7}
>>> a.keys()
['Age', 'Name']
```

```
dict.pop(key[,default])
```
If `key` is in the dictionary, remove it and return its value, else return `default`. If `default` is **not given** and `key` is not in the dictionary, a `KeyError` is raised.

```
>>> a={'Gender':'Female','Age':7,'Hair color':None,'Name':'Zara'}
>>> a.pop('Age',15)
```

```
7
>>> a.pop('Age',15)
15
>>> a
{'Gender': 'Female', 'Hair color': None, 'Name': 'Zara'}
```

dict.popitem()
Remove and return an arbitrary key-value pair from the dictionary. If the dictionary is empty, calling popitem() raises an KeyError exception.

```
>>> a={'Gender':'Female','Age':7,'Hair color':None,'Name':'Zara'}
>>> a.popitem()
('Gender', 'Female')
>>> a.popitem()
('Age', 7)
>>> a
{'Hair color': None, 'Name': 'Zara'}
```

dict.setdefault(key[,default])
If key is in the dictionary, return its value. If not, insert key with a value of default and return default. The default defaults to None.

```
>>> a={'Name':'Zara','Age':7}
>>> a.setdefault('Age',15)
7
>>> a.setdefault('Gender','Female')
'Female'
>>> a.setdefault('Hair color')
>>> a
{'Gender': 'Female', 'Age': 7, 'Hair color': None, 'Name': 'Zara'}
```

dict.update([other])
Update the dictionary with the key-value pairs from other, overwriting existing keys, and returns None. The method accepts either another dictionary object or an iterable of key-value pairs (as tuples or other iterables of length two). If keyword arguments are specified, the dictionary is then updated with those key-value pairs.

```
>>> dict1={'Name':'Zara','Age':7}
>>> dict2={'Gender':'female'}
>>> dict1.update(dict2)
>>> dict1.update(hair_color='black',eye_color='blue')
>>> dict1
{'eye_color': 'blue', 'Gender': 'female', 'Age': 7, 'Name': 'Zara', 'hair_color': 'black'}
```

dict.values()
Return list of dictionary values.

```
>>> a={'Name':'Zara','Age':7}
>>> a.values()
[7, 'Zara']
```

Chapter 5
MODULES AND PACKAGES

As the program gets longer, it is a good option to split it into several files for easier maintenance. There might also be a situation when the programmer wants to use a handy function that is used in several programs without copying its definition into each program. To support such scenarios, Python has a way to put definitions in a file and use them in a script or in an interactive instance of the interpreter.

5.1. Module

A module is a file containing Python definitions and statements. The file name is the module name with the suffix *.py* appended. Definitions from a module can be imported into other modules. For instance, consider a script file called "fibo.py" in the current directory with the following code.

```
# Fibonacci numbers module

def fib(n):      # write Fibonacci series up to n
    a,b=0,1
    while b<n:
        print b,
        a,b=b,a+b

def fib2(n):     # return Fibonacci series up to n
    result=[]
    a,b=0,1
    while b<n:
        result.append(b)
        a,b=b,a+b
    return result
```

Now on the Python interpreter, import this module with the following command:

```
>>> import fibo
```

Within a module, the module's name (as a string) is available as the value of the global variable __name__:

```
>>> fibo.__name__
'fibo'
```

Use the module's name to access its functions:

```
>>> fibo.fib(1000)
1 1 2 3 5 8 13 21 34 55 89 144 233 377 610 987
>>> fibo.fib2(1000)
[1, 1, 2, 3, 5, 8, 13, 21, 34, 55, 89, 144, 233, 377, 610, 987]
```

If it is intended to use a function often, assign it to a local name:

```
>>> Fibonacci=fibo.fib
>>> Fibonacci(500)
1 1 2 3 5 8 13 21 34 55 89 144 233 377
```

5.1.1. More on modules

A module can contain executable statements as well as function definitions. These statements are intended to initialize the module. They are executed only the first time the module name is encountered in an `import` statement; they also run if the file is executed as a script.

Each module has its own private symbol table, which is used as the global symbol table by all functions defined in the module. Thus, the author of a module can use global variables in the module without worrying about accidental clashes with a user's global variables.

Modules can import other modules. It is customary but not required to place all import statements at the beginning of a module. The imported module names are placed in the importing module's global symbol table.

There is a variant of the `import` statement that import specific names from a module directly into the importing module's symbol table. For example, specific attributes of `fibo` module are imported in local namespace as:

```
>>> from fibo import fib, fib2
>>> fib(500)
1 1 2 3 5 8 13 21 34 55 89 144 233 377
```

This does not introduce the module name from which the imports are taken in the local symbol table (so in the example, `fibo` is not defined).

There is even a variant to import all names that a module defines:

```
>>> from fibo import *
>>> fib(500)
1 1 2 3 5 8 13 21 34 55 89 144 233 377
```

This imports all names except those beginning with an underscore (_).

Note that in general, the practice of importing * from a module or package is discouraged, since it often causes poorly readable code. However, it is okay to use it to save typing in interactive session. For efficiency reason, each module is only imported once per interpreter session. If changes are made in many modules, it is a wise approach to restart the interpreter or if it is just one module that needs to be tested interactively, use `reload()`, e.g. `reload(modulename)`.

5.1.2. Executing modules as scripts

When a Python module is run at command prompt

```
$ python fibo.py <arguments>
```

the code in the module will be executed, just as if it imported, but with the __name__ set to __main__. That means, by adding the following code at the end of the module:

```
if __name__ == "__main__":
    import sys
    fib(int(sys.argv[1]))
```

the file is made usable as a script as well as an importable module, because the code that parses the command line only runs if the module is executed as the "main" file:

```
$ python fibo.py 50
1 1 2 3 5 8 13 21 34
```

5.1.3. The Module Search Path

When a module named `fibo` is imported, the interpreter first searches for a built-in module with that name. If not found, it then searches for a file named `fibo.py` in a list of directories given by the variable `sys.path`. The variable `sys.path` is initialized from some of these locations:
- The current directory.
- `PYTHONPATH` environment variable (a list of directory names, with the same syntax as the shell variable `PATH`).

After initialization, Python programs can modify `sys.path`. The directory containing the script being run is placed at the beginning of the search path, ahead of the standard library path. This means that scripts in that directory will be loaded instead of modules of the same name in the library directory.

5.1.4. Math module

Python has `math` module and it is always available. The functions provided in this module cannot be used with complex numbers; use the functions of the same name from the `cmath` module for support of complex numbers. The distinction between functions which support complex numbers and those which does not is made since most users do not want to learn quite as much mathematics as required to understand complex numbers. Except when explicitly noted otherwise, all functions return float values.

5.1.4.1. Constants

`math.pi`
The mathematical constant π.

```
>>> math.pi
3.141592653589793
```

```
math.e
```
The mathematical constant `e`.

```
>>> math.e
2.718281828459045
```

5.1.4.2. Number-theoretic and representation functions

```
math.ceil(x)
```
Return the ceiling of `x` as a float, the smallest integer value greater than or equal to `x`.

```
>>> import math
>>> math.ceil(-3.2)
-3.0
>>> math.ceil(3.2)
4.0
```

```
math.copysign(x,y)
```
Return `x` with the sign of `y`.

```
>>> math.copysign(5.1,-2.8)
-5.1
>>> math.copysign(-5.1,2.8)
5.1
```

```
math.fabs(x)
```
Return the absolute value of `x`.

```
>>> math.fabs(-4.2)
4.2
```

```
math.factorial(x)
```
Return `x` factorial. Raises `ValueError`, if `x` is not integral or is negative.

```
>>> math.factorial(5)
120
>>> math.factorial(-5)
Traceback (most recent call last):
  File "<stdin>", line 1, in <module>
ValueError: factorial() not defined for negative values
```

```
math.floor(x)
```
Return the largest integer value less than or equal to `x` as a float.

```
>>> math.floor(-3.2)
-4.0
>>> math.floor(3.2)
3.0
```

```
math.fmod(x,y)
```
Return remainder of a division expression. Note that the Python expression `x%y` may not return the same result. The result of `fmod(x,y)` has same sign as `x`, while `x%y` returns a result with the sign of `y` instead.

```
>>> math.fmod(5.0,-2.0)
1.0
>>> 5.0%-2.0
-1.0
>>> math.fmod(-5.0,2.0)
-1.0
>>> -5.0%2.0
1.0
```

Consider the following interesting scenario.

```
>>> math.fmod(-1e-100,1e100)
-1e-100
>>> -1e-100 % 1e100
1e+100
```

It can be observed that `fmod(-1e-100,1e100)` returns `-1e-100`, but the result of Python's `-1e-100%1e100` is `1e100-1e-100`, which cannot be represented exactly as a float, and rounds to the surprising `1e100`. For this reason, function `fmod()` is generally preferred when working with floats, while Python's `x%y` is preferred when working with integers.

```
math.frexp(x)
```
Return the mantissa and exponent of `x` as the pair `(m,e)`. The `m` is a float and `e` is an integer such that $x = m \times 2^e$ exactly. If `x` is zero, returns (0.0, 0), otherwise `0.5<=abs(m)<1`.

```
>>> math.frexp(4.0)
(0.5, 3)
>>> 0.5*2**3
4.0
>>> math.frexp(0.1)
(0.8, -3)
>>> 0.8*2**-3
0.1
>>> math.frexp(-4.0)
(-0.5, 3)
>>> -0.5*2**3
-4.0
```

```
math.fsum(iterable)
```
Return an accurate floating point sum of values in the iterable.

```
>>> math.fsum([.1, .1, .1, .1, .1, .1, .1, .1, .1, .1])
```

```
1.0
```

```
math.isinf(x)
```
Check if the float `x` is positive or negative infinity.

```
>>> a=1e+300
>>> a
1e+300
>>> math.isinf(1e+300)
False
>>> a=1e+310
>>> a
inf
>>> math.isinf(1e+310)
True
```

Calculating an exponent with floating point values, in particular, raises `OverflowError` instead of preserving the `inf` result.

```
>>> a=10.0**310

Traceback (most recent call last):
  File "<pyshell#1>", line 1, in <module>
    a=10.0**310
OverflowError: (34, 'Result too large')
```

```
math.isnan(x)
```
Check if the float `x` is a nan (not a number). nan does not compare as equal to any value, even itself, so nan should be checked using `isnan()` function.

```
>>> a=1e+310
>>> a
inf
>>> b=a/a
>>> b
nan
>>> math.isnan(a)
False
>>> math.isnan(b)
True
```

```
math.ldexp(x,i)
```
Return `x*(2**i)`. This function is reverse of function `frexp()`.

```
>>> math.ldexp(-0.5,3)
-4.0
>>> -0.5*2**3
-4.0
```

```
>>> math.ldexp(0.8,-3)
0.1
>>> 0.8*2**-3
0.1
```

`math.modf(x)`
Return the fractional and integer parts of x. Both results carry the sign of x and are floats.

```
>>> math.modf(1.5)
(0.5, 1.0)
>>> math.modf(-1.5)
(-0.5, -1.0)
```

`math.trunc(x)`
Return the real value x truncated to an integer.

```
>>> math.trunc(93.2508)
93
>>> math.trunc(-93.2508)
-93
```

5.1.4.3. Power and logarithmic functions

`math.exp(x)`
Return e^x.

```
>>> math.e**-3.2
0.040762203978366622
>>> math.pow(math.e,-3.2)
0.040762203978366622
>>> math.exp(-3.2)
0.040762203978366621
```

`math.expm1(x)`
Return $e^x - 1$. For small floats x, the subtraction in `exp(x)-1` can result in a significant loss of precision; the `expm1()` function provides a way to compute this quantity to full precision:

```
>>> x=0.0000000000000000000000001
>>> math.exp(x)-1
0.0
>>> math.expm1(x)
1e-25
```

`math.log(x[,base])`
With one argument, return the natural logarithm of x (to base e). With two arguments, return the logarithm of x to the given `base`, calculated as `log(x)/log(base)`.

```
>>> math.log(9)
```

```
2.1972245773362196
>>> math.log(9,2)
3.1699250014423126
```

`math.log1p(x)`
Return the natural logarithm of 1+x (base e). The result is calculated in a way which is accurate for x near zero.

```
>>> x=0.0000000000000000000000001
>>> x
1e-25
>>> 1+x
1.0
>>> math.log(1+x)
0.0
>>> math.log1p(x)
1e-25
```

`math.log10(x)`
Return the base-10 logarithm of x. This is usually more accurate than `log(x,10)`.

```
>>> math.log10(100)
2.0
>>> math.log10(10000)
4.0
```

`math.pow(x,y)`
Return x raised to the power y. In particular, `pow(1.0,x)` and `pow(x,0.0)` always return 1.0, even when x is a zero or a NaN. If both x and y are finite, x is negative, and y is not an integer then `pow(x,y)` is undefined, and raises `ValueError`.

```
>>> math.pow(9.0,0.5)
3.0
>>> math.pow(-9.0,0.5)
Traceback (most recent call last):
  File "<stdin>", line 1, in <module>
ValueError: math domain error
```

Unlike the built-in `**` operator, `math.pow()` converts both its arguments to type float.

`math.sqrt(x)`
Return the square root of x. Computing the square roots of negative numbers requires complex numbers, which are not handled by `math` module. Any attempt to calculate a square root of a negative value results in `ValueError`.

```
>>> math.sqrt(9.0)
3.0
>>> math.sqrt(-9.0)
```

```
Traceback (most recent call last):
  File "<pyshell#62>", line 1, in <module>
    math.sqrt(-9.0)
ValueError: math domain error
```

5.1.4.4. Trigonometric functions

```
math.acos(x)
```
Return the arc cosine of x, in radians.

```
>>> math.acos(0.5)
1.0471975511965979
```

```
math.asin(x)
```
Return the arc sine of x, in radians.

```
>>> math.asin(0.5)
0.5235987755982989
```

```
math.atan(x)
```
Return the arc tangent of x, in radians.

```
>>> math.atan(0.5)
0.4636476090008061
```

```
math.atan2(y,x)
```
Return `atan(y/x)`, in radians. The result is between −π and π. The vector in the plane from the origin to point `(x,y)` makes this angle with the positive X axis. The point of `atan2()` is that the signs of both inputs are known to it, so it can compute the correct quadrant for the angle. For example, `atan(1)` and `atan2(1,1)` are both $\pi/4$, but `atan2(-1,-1)` is $-3\pi/4$.

```
>>> math.atan(1.0)
0.7853981633974483
>>> math.pi/4
0.7853981633974483
```

```
math.cos(x)
```
Return the cosine of x radians.

```
>>> math.cos(0.7853981633974483)
0.7071067811865476
```

```
math.hypot(x,y)
```
Return the Euclidean distance, $\sqrt{x^2 + y^2}$. This is the length of the vector from the origin to point `(x,y)`.

```
>>> math.hypot(3.0,4.0)
5.0
```

```
math.sin(x)
```
Return the sine of x radians.

```
>>> math.sin(0.7853981633974483)
0.7071067811865475
```

```
math.tan(x)
```
Return the tangent of x radians.

```
>>> math.tan(0.7853981633974483)
0.9999999999999999
```

5.1.4.5. Angular conversion

```
math.degrees(x)
```
Converts angle x from radians to degrees.

```
>>> math.degrees(1.5707963267948966)
90.0
>>> 1.5707963267948966*180/math.pi
90.0
```

```
math.radians(x)
```
Converts angle x from degrees to radians.

```
>>> math.radians(90)
1.5707963267948966
>>> (90*math.pi)/180
1.5707963267948966
```

5.1.4.6. Hyperbolic functions

```
math.acosh(x)
```
Return the inverse hyperbolic cosine of x.

```
>>> math.cosh(1.0)
1.5430806348152437
```

```
math.asinh(x)
```
Return the inverse hyperbolic sine of x.

```
>>> math.asinh(1.0)
0.8813735870195429
```

```
math.atanh(x)
```
Return the inverse hyperbolic tangent of x.

```
>>> math.atanh(0.8)
1.0986122886681098
```

```
math.cosh(x)
```
Return the hyperbolic cosine of x.

```
>>> math.cosh(0.7853981633974483)
1.3246090892520057
```

```
math.sinh(x)
```
Return the hyperbolic sine of x.

```
>>> math.sinh(0.7853981633974483)
0.8686709614860095
```

```
math.tanh(x)
```
Return the hyperbolic tangent of x.

```
>>> math.tanh(0.7853981633974483)
0.6557942026326724
```

5.1.4.7. Special functions

```
math.erf(x)
```
Return the error function at x.

```
>>> math.erf(0.25)
0.2763263901682369
```

```
math.erfc(x)
```
Return the complementary error function at x i.e. 1-erf(x).

```
>>> math.erfc(0.25)
0.7236736098317631
```

```
math.gamma(x)
```
Return the gamma function at x.

```
>>> math.gamma(5.5)
52.34277778455352
```

```
math.lgamma(x)
```
Return the natural logarithm of the absolute value of the gamma function at x.

```
>>> math.lgamma(5.5)
3.9578139676187165
```

5.1.5. Random module

This module implements pseudo-random number generators for various distributions. Almost all module functions depend on the basic function `random()`, which generates a random float uniformly in the semi-open range `[0.0,1.0)`. Python uses the "Mersenne Twister" as the core generator. However, Mersenne Twister being completely deterministic, it is not suitable for all purposes, and is completely unsuitable for cryptographic purposes.

5.1.5.1. Functions for integers

`random.randrange(stop)`

Return a randomly selected integer element from range `(0,stop)`.

```
>>> random.randrange(88)
17
>>> random.randrange(-88)

Traceback (most recent call last):
  File "<pyshell#1>", line 1, in <module>
    random.randrange(-88)
  File "C:\Python27\lib\random.py", line 191, in randrange
    raise ValueError, "empty range for randrange()"
ValueError: empty range for randrange()
```

`random.randrange(start,stop[,step])`
Return a randomly selected integer element from range `(start,stop,step)`.

```
>>> random.randrange(3,100,5)
83
```

`random.randint(a,b)`
Return a random integer N such that a<=N<=b.

```
>>> random.randint(5, 86)
70
```

5.1.5.2. Functions for sequences

`random.choice(seq)`
Return a random element from the non-empty sequence `seq`. If `seq` is empty, raises `IndexError`.

```
>>> random.choice('abcdefghij')
'e'
>>> random.choice(['aa','bb','cc',11,22])
```

```
'cc'
```

```
random.shuffle(x[,random])
```
Shuffle the sequence `x` in place. The optional argument `random` is a 0-argument function returning a random float in `[0.0,1.0)`; by default, this is the function `random()`.

```
>>> items=[1,2,3,4,5,6,7]
>>> random.shuffle(items)
>>> items
[4, 7, 2, 6, 3, 5, 1]
```

```
random.sample(population,k)
```
Return a `k` length list of unique elements chosen from the `population` sequence; used for random sampling without replacement. Return a new list containing elements from the `population`, while leaving the original `population` unchanged. If the `population` contain repeating elements, then each occurrence is a possible selection in the sample.

```
>>> random.sample([1,2,3,4,5],3)
[4, 5, 1]
```

To choose a sample from a range of integers, use an `xrange()` object as an argument. This is especially fast and space efficient for sampling from a large population.

```
>>> random.sample(xrange(10000000),5)
[2445367, 2052603, 975267, 3021085, 6098369]
```

5.1.5.3. Functions for floating point values

```
random.random()
```
Return the next random floating point number in the range `[0.0,1.0)`.

```
>>> random.random()
0.6229016948897019
```

```
random.uniform(a,b)
```
Return a random floating point number N, such that a<=N<=b for a<=b and b<=N<=a for b<a.

```
>>> random.uniform(0.5,0.6)
0.5795193565565696
```

```
random.triangular(low,high,mode)
```
Return a random floating point number N such that low<=N<=high and with the specified `mode` between those bounds. The `low` and `high` bounds default to 0 and 1, respectively. The `mode` argument defaults to the midpoint between the bounds, giving a symmetric distribution.

```
>>> random.triangular(2.8,10.9,7.5)
6.676127015045406
```

```
random.betavariate(alpha,beta)
```
Beta distribution; conditions of the parameters are `alpha>0` and `beta>0`. Returned values range between 0 and 1.

```
>>> random.betavariate(2.5,1.0)
0.543590525336106
```

```
random.expovariate(lambd)
```
Exponential distribution; `lambd` is 1.0 divided by the desired mean. It should be nonzero. Returned values range from 0 to positive infinity; if `lambd` is positive, and from negative infinity to 0, if `lambd` is negative.

```
>>> random.expovariate(0.5)
1.5287594548764503
```

```
random.gammavariate(alpha,beta)
```
Gamma distribution (not the gamma function). Conditions of the parameters are `alpha>0` and `beta>0`.

```
>>> random.gammavariate(1.3, 0.5)
0.5893587279305473
```

```
random.gauss(mu,sigma)
```
Gaussian distribution; `mu` is the mean, and `sigma` is the standard deviation. This is slightly faster than the `normalvariate()` function defined below.

```
>>> random.gauss(0.5,1.9)
-1.8886943114939512
```

```
random.lognormvariate(mu,sigma)
```
Log normal distribution; if natural logarithm of this distribution is taken, a normal distribution with mean `mu` and standard deviation `sigma` is received. `mu` can have any value, and `sigma` must be greater than zero.

```
>>> random.lognormvariate(0.5,1.9)
4.621063728160664
```

```
random.normalvariate(mu,sigma)
```
Normal distribution; `mu` is the mean, and `sigma` is the standard deviation.

```
>>> random.normalvariate(0.5,1.9)
1.6246107732503214
```

```
random.vonmisesvariate(mu,kappa)
```

mu is the mean angle, expressed in radians between 0 and 2π, and kappa is the concentration parameter, which must be greater than or equal to zero. If kappa is equal to zero, this distribution reduces to a uniform random angle over the range 0 to 2π.

```
>>> random.vonmisesvariate(0.5,1.9)
-0.4664831190641767
```

random.paretovariate(alpha)
Pareto distribution; alpha is the shape parameter.

```
>>> random.paretovariate(0.5)
60.471412103322585
```

random.weibullvariate(alpha,beta)
Weibull distribution; alpha is the scale parameter and beta is the shape parameter.

```
>>> random.weibullvariate(0.5,1.9)
0.9229896561284915
```

5.1.5.4. Alternative generators
Apart from Mersenne Twister, there are more core random number generator, such as generator based on "Wichmann-Hill" algorithm.

```
>>> rnd=random.WichmannHill()
>>> rnd.random()
0.4065226158909223
>>>
>>> rnd=random.SystemRandom()
>>> rnd.random()
0.46579102190832355
```

5.2. Package
As discussed previously, functions and global variables usually reside inside a module. There might be a scenario where organizing modules needs to be done. That is where packages come into the picture. Packages are just folders of modules with a special "__init__.py" file, that intimate Python that this folder is special because it contains Python modules. In the simplest case, "__init__.py" can just be an empty file, but it can also execute initialization code for the package or set the __all__ variable, described later.

Suppose there is an objective to design a collection of modules (a "package") for the uniform handling of sound files and sound data. There are many different sound file formats (usually recognized by their extension, for example: *.wav*, *.aiff*, *.au*), so it might be needed to create and maintain a growing collection of modules for the conversion between the various file formats. There are also many different operations that are needed to perform on sound data (such as mixing, adding echo, applying an equalizer function, creating an artificial stereo effect), so there will be numerous modules to perform these operations. Here is a schematic structure for the package:

```
sound/                          Top-level package
    __init__.py                 Initialize the sound package

    formats/                    Subpackage for file format conversions
            __init__.py
            wavread.py
            wavwrite.py
            aiffread.py
            aiffwrite.py
            auread.py
            auwrite.py
            ...
    effects/                    Subpackage for sound effects
            __init__.py
            echo.py
            surround.py
            reverse.py
            ...
    filters/                    Subpackage for filters
            __init__.py
            equalizer.py
            vocoder.py
            karaoke.py
            ...
```

When importing the package, Python searches through the directories on `sys.path` looking for the package sub-directory. Users of the package can import individual modules from the package, for example:

```
import sound.effects.echo
```

This loads the sub-module `sound.effects.echo`. It must be referenced with its full name.

```
sound.effects.echo.echofilter(input,output,delay=0.7,atten=4)
```

An alternative way of importing the sub-module is:

```
from sound.effects import echo
```

This loads the sub-module `echo`, and makes it available without its package prefix, so it can be used as follows:

```
echo.echofilter(input,output,delay=0.7,atten=4)
```

Yet another variation is to import the desired function or variable directly:

```
from sound.effects.echo import echofilter
```

This makes `echofilter()` directly available:

```
echofilter(input,output,delay=0.7,atten=4)
```

Note that when using `from package import item`, the `item` can be either a sub-module (or sub-package) of the package, or some other name defined in the package, like a function, class or variable. The import statement first tests whether the `item` is defined in the package; if not, it assumes it is a module and attempts to load it. If it fails to find it, an `ImportError` exception is raised. Contrarily, when using syntax like `import item.subitem.subsubitem`, each item except for the last must be a package; the last item can be a module or a package but cannot be a class or function or variable defined in the previous item.

5.2.1. Importing * from a package

What happens when the programmer writes `from sound.effects import *`? Ideally, one would hope that this somehow goes out to the file system, finds which sub-modules are present in the package, and imports them all. This could take a long time.

The only solution is for the package author to provide an explicit index of the package. The import statement uses the following convention: if a package's `__init__.py` code defines a list named `__all__`, it is taken to be the list of module names that should be imported when `from package import *` is encountered. It is up to the package author to keep this list up-to-date when a new version of the package is released. Package authors may also decide not to support it, if they does not see a use for importing * from their package. For example, the file `sounds/effects/__init__.py` could contain the following code:

```
__all__ = ["echo", "surround", "reverse"]
```

This would mean that `from sound.effects import *` would import the three named sub-modules of the `sound` package.

If `__all__` is not defined, the statement `from sound.effects import *` does not import all sub-modules from the package `sound.effects` into the current namespace; it only ensures that the package `sound.effects` has been imported (possibly running any initialization code in `__init__.py`) and then imports whatever names are defined in the package. This includes any names defined (and sub-modules explicitly loaded) by `__init__.py`. It also includes any sub-modules of the package that were explicitly loaded by previous import statements.

Remember, there is nothing wrong with using `from Package import specific_submodule`. In fact, this is the recommended notation, unless the importing module need to use sub-modules with the same name from different packages.

5.2.2. Intra-package references

The sub-modules often need to refer to each other. For example, the `surround` module might use the `echo` module. In fact, such references are so common that the `import` statement first looks in the containing package before looking in the standard module search path. Thus, the `surround` module can simply use `import echo` or `from echo import echofilter`. If the imported module is not found in the current package (the package of which the current module is a sub-module), the `import` statement looks for a top-level module with the given name.

When packages are structured into sub-packages (as with the `sound` package in the example), the programmer can use absolute imports to refer to sub-modules of siblings packages. For example, if the module `sound.filters.vocoder` needs to use the `echo` module in the `sound.effects` package, it can use `from sound.effects import echo`.

Starting with Python 2.5, in addition to the implicit relative imports described above, the programmer can write explicit relative imports with the `from module import name` form of `import` statement. These explicit relative imports use leading dots to indicate the current and parent packages involved in the relative import. From the `surround` module for example, you might use:

```
from . import echo
from .. import formats
from ..filters import equalizer
```

5.2.3.   Packages in multiple directories

Package support one more special attribute, __path__. This is initialized to be a list containing the name of the directory holding the package's __init__.py before the code in that file is executed. This variable can be modified, doing so affect future searches for modules and sub-packages contained in the package. While this feature is not often needed, it can be used to extend the set of modules found in a package.

```
>>> import numpy
>>> numpy.__path__
['C:\\Python27\\lib\\site-packages\\numpy']
```

Chapter 6
OBJECT ORIENTED PROGRAMMING

Object-oriented programming (OOP) is a programming paradigm that represents concepts as "objects", that have attributes which describe the object in the form of data attributes and associated procedures known as methods. As mentioned in chapter 1, Python is an OOP language. In Python, class form the basis of OOP. Some of the features of OOP language are:
- Inheritence
- Polymorphism
- Encapsulation

Some of the advantages of OOP approach are:
- Reusability: A part of a code can be reused for accommodating new functionalities with little or no changes.
- Maintenance: If some modification is made in base class, the effect gets reflected automatically into the derived class, thus, the code maintenance is significantly less hectic.
- Faster output: With organized and methodical coding, there is little room for error, and as a result programmer can work comfortably, resulting in fast and efficient output.

6.1. Class
A class is the particular object type created by executing a class statement. Class objects are used as templates to create instance objects, which embodies the attributes: the "data attributes" and "methods", specific to a data type. A class definition is given below:

```
classdef      ::=   "class" classname [inheritance] ":" suite
inheritance ::=   "(" [expression_list] ")"
classname    ::=   identifier
```

The above class definition might seem alien, it will become more clear with the progress of this chapter. The simplest form of class definition looks like:

```
class ClassName:
    <statement-1>
    .
    .
    .
    <statement-N>
```

The following example gives a glimpse of how a class is defined.

```
>>> class Output:
...     def Display(self):
...         print 'This is a class example.'
...
>>> x=Output()
```

```
>>> x.Display()
This is a class example.
```

Like function definition (`def` statements), the class definition (`Output` in the above example) must be executed before they have any effect. In practice, the statements inside a class definition will usually be function (or more specifically "method") definitions (`Display()` in the above example), but other statements are allowed. The function definitions inside a class normally have a peculiar form of argument list, dictated by the calling conventions for methods (discussed later).

Creation of a class definition also creates a new namespace, and used as the local scope, thus all assignments to local variables go into this new namespace.

6.1.1. Method

A method is a function that belongs to an object. In Python, the term "method" is not unique to class instance, other object types can have methods as well. For example, list objects have methods, namely, append, insert, remove, sort, and so on.

Usually in a class, the method is defined inside its body. If called as an attribute of an instance of that class, the method will get the instance object as its first argument (which is usually called `self`). Self is merely a conventional name for the first argument of a method. For example, a method defined as `meth(self,a,b,c)` should be called as `x.meth(a,b,c)` for an instance `x` of the class in which the definition occurs; the called method will think it is called as `meth(x,a,b,c)`. The idea of `self` was borrowed from "Modula-3" programming language.

It is not necessary that the function definition is textually enclosed in the class definition; assigning a function object to a local variable in the class is also fine. For example:

```
>>> def f1(self,x,y):
...        return min(x,x+y)
...
>>> class test_class:
...        aa=f1
...        def bb(self):
...            return 'hello world'
...        cc=bb
...
>>>
```

Here `aa`, `bb` and `cc` are all attributes of class `test_class` that refer to function objects, and consequently, they are all methods of instances of class `test_class`; `cc` being exactly equivalent to `bb`. Note that this practice usually confuses the reader of the program.

Usually, Python use methods for some functionality (e.g. `list.index()`), but functions for other (e.g. `len(list)`). The major reason is history; functions were used for those operations that were generic for a group of types and which were intended to work even for objects that did not have methods at all (e.g. tuples). In fact, implementing `len()`, `max()`, `min()` etc. as built-in functions has actually less code than implementing them as methods for each type. One can quibble about individual cases, but it is part of Python, and it is too late to make such fundamental changes now. The functions have to remain to avoid massive code breakage.

6.1.2. Class object

When a class definition is created, a "class object" is also created. The class object is basically a wrapper around the contents of the namespace created by the class definition. Class object support two kinds of operations: "attribute reference" and "instantiation".

6.1.2.1. Attribute reference

Attribute references use the standard syntax used for all attribute references in Python: `obj.name`. Valid attribute names are all the names that were in the class's namespace, when the class object was created. So, if the class definition looked like this:

```
>>> class MyClass:
...     """A simple example class"""
...     i=12345
...     def f(self):
...         return 'hello world'
...
>>> MyClass.i
12345
>>> MyClass.__doc__
'A simple example class'
```

then `MyClass.i` and `MyClass.f` are valid attribute references, returning an integer and a method object, respectively. The value of `MyClass.i` can also be change by assignment. The attribute `__doc__` is also a valid attribute, returning the `docstring` belonging to the class.

```
>>> type(MyClass)
<type 'classobj'>
```

From the above expression, it can be noticed that `MyClass` is a class object.

6.1.2.2. Instantiation

A class object can be called to yield a class instance. Class instantiation uses function notation. For example (assuming the above class `MyClass`):

```
x=MyClass()
```

creates a new instance of the class `MyClass`, and assigns this object to the local variable `x`.

```
>>> type(MyClass())
<type 'instance'>
>>> type(x)
<type 'instance'>
```

Many classes like to create objects with instances customized to a specific initial state. Therefore, a class may define a special method named __init__(), like this:

```
def __init__(self):
    self.data=[]
```

When a class defines an __init__() method, class instantiation automatically invokes __init__() for the newly created class instance. So in this example, a new, initialized instance can be obtained by:

```
x=MyClass()
```

Of course, the __init__() method may have arguments for greater flexibility. In that case, arguments given to the class instantiation operator are passed on to __init__(). For example,

```
>>> class Complex:
...      def __init__(self,realpart,imagpart):
...          self.r=realpart
...          self.i=imagpart
...
>>> x=Complex(3.0,-4.5)
>>> x.r,x.i
(3.0, -4.5)
```

6.1.3. Instance object
The only operation that done using class instance object x is attribute references. There are two kinds of valid attribute names: "data attribute" and "method".

Data attribute correspond to variable of a class instance. Data attributes need not be declared; like local variables, they spring into existence when they are first assigned to. For example, if x is the instance of MyClass (created before), the following piece of code will print the value 16, without leaving a trace:

```
>>> x.counter=1
>>> while x.counter<10:
...      x.counter=x.counter*2
...
>>> print x.counter
16
>>> del x.counter
```

The other kind of instance attribute reference is a method. Any function object that is a class attribute defines a method for instances of that class. So, x.f is a valid method reference, since MyClass.f is a function.

[148]

6.1.4. Method object

In the `MyClass` example, `x.f` is a method object, and `x.f()` returns the string `'hello world'`. The call `x.f()` is exactly equivalent to `MyClass.f(x)`. In general, calling a method with a list of `n` arguments is equivalent to calling the corresponding function with an argument list that is created by inserting the method's object before the first argument

```
>>> x.f()
'hello world'
>>> x.f()==MyClass.f(x)
True
```

The method object can be stored and can be called later.

```
>>> xf=x.f
>>> print xf()
hello world
>>> type(xf)
<type 'instancemethod'>
```

6.1.5. Pre-defined attributes

Class and class instance objects has some pre-defined attributes:

6.1.5.1. Class object

Some pre-defined attributes of class object are:

__name__
This attribute give the class name.

```
>>> MyClass.__name__
'MyClass'
```

__module__
This attribute give the module name in which the class was defined.

```
>>> MyClass.__module__
'__main__'
```

__dict__
A class has a namespace implemented by a dictionary object. Class attribute references are translated to lookups in this dictionary, e.g., `MyClass.i` is translated to `MyClass.__dict__["i"]`.

```
>>> MyClass.__dict__
{'i': 12345, '__module__': '__main__', '__doc__': 'A simple example
class', 'f': <function f at 0x0640A070>}
```

__bases__
This attribute give the tuple (possibly empty or a singleton) containing the base classes.

```
>>> MyClass.__bases__
()
```

__doc__

This attribute give the class documentation string, or `None`, if not defined.

```
>>> MyClass.__doc__
'A simple example class'
```

6.1.5.2. Class instance object

Some pre-defined attributes of class instance object are:

__dict__

This give attribute dictionary of class instance.

```
>>> x.__dict__
{}
```

__class__

This give the instance's class.

```
>>> x.__class__
<class __main__.MyClass at 0x063DA880>
```

6.1.6. Customizing attribute access

The following are some methods that can be defined to customize the meaning of attribute access for class instance.

`object.__getattr__(self,name)`
Called when an attribute lookup does not find the attribute `name`. This method should return the (computed) attribute value or raise an `AttributeError` exception. Note that, if the attribute is found through the normal mechanism, `__getattr__()` is not called.

```
>>> class HiddenMembers:
...       def __getattr__(self,name):
...           return "You don't get to see "+name
...
>>> h=HiddenMembers()
>>> h.anything
"You don't get to see anything"
```

`object.__setattr__(self,name,value)`
Called when an attribute assignment is attempted. The `name` is the attribute name and `value` is the value to be assigned to it. Each class, of course, comes with a default `__setattr__`, which simply set the value of the variable, but that can be overridden.

```
>>> class Unchangable:
...     def __setattr__(self,name,value):
...         print "Nice try"
...
>>> u=Unchangable()
>>> u.x=9
Nice try
>>> u.x
 Traceback (most recent call last):
  File "<stdin>", line 1, in ?
AttributeError: Unchangable instance has no attribute 'x'
```

object.__delattr__(self,name)
Like __setattr__(), but for attribute deletion instead of assignment. This should only be
implemented if del obj.name is meaningful for the object.

```
>>> class Permanent:
...     def __delattr__(self,name):
...         print name,"cannot be deleted"
...
>>> p=Permanent()
>>> p.x=9
>>> del p.x
x cannot be deleted
>>> p.x
9
```

6.1.7. Class example

Till now, some basic concepts of class has been discussed. The following example "ClassExample.py"
defines a class Person, which handles name and age of multiple individuals.

```
class Person:
    """The program handles individual's data"""
    population=0

    def __init__(self,Name,Age):
        """Initializes the data."""
        self.name=Name
        self.age=Age
        Person.population+=1

    def __del__(self):
        """Deleting the data."""
        print('Record of {0} is being removed'.format(self.name))
        Person.population-=1

    def AgeDetails(self):
        '''Age details:'''
        print('{0} is {1} years old'.format(self.name,self.age))
```

```
    def Records(cls):
        """Print number of records."""
        print('There are {0} records'.format(cls.population))

    records=classmethod(Records)

print Person.__doc__
record1=Person('Ram',26)
print Person.AgeDetails.__doc__
record1.AgeDetails()
Person.records()
record2=Person('Ahmed',20)
print record2.AgeDetails.__doc__
record2.AgeDetails()
record2.records()
record3=Person('John',22)
print Person.AgeDetails.__doc__
record3.AgeDetails()
Person.records()
del record1,record2
Person.records()
```

The output is:

```
The program handles individual's data
Age details:
Ram is 26 years old
There are 1 records
Age details:
Ahmed is 20 years old
There are 2 records
Age details:
John is 22 years old
There are 3 records
Record of Ram is being removed
Record of Ahmed is being removed
There are 1 records
```

Variables defined in the class definition are class variables (population is a class variable); they are shared by all instances. To create instance variables (name and age are instance variables), they can be initialized in a method, e.g. self.name=value. Both class and instance variables are accessible through the notation self.name, and an instance variable hides a class variable with the same name when accessed in this way. Therefore, the class variable population is better referred as Person.population, and not self.population. The instance variables name and age are referred as self.name and self.age, respectively.

The `Records` is a method that belongs to the class and not to the instance. This is done by using `classmethod()` built-in function. A class method receives the class as implicit first argument, just like an instance method receives the instance. The class method can be called either on the class (`Person.records()`) or on an instance (`record2.records()`). The instance is ignored except for its class.

The `__doc__` attribute is used to access docstrings of class (`Person.__doc__`) and methods (`record2.AgeDetails.__doc__`).

The `__del__()` method is called when an instance is about to be destroyed. This is also called a destructor.

6.2. Inheritence

A class can be based on one or more other classes, called its "base class(es)". It then inherits the data attributes and methods of its base classes. This is called "inheritance", and the class which inherits from the base class is called "derived class". A class definition first evaluates the inheritance list, if present. A simple form of derived class definition looks like:

```
class DerivedClassName(BaseClassName):
    <statement-1>
    .
    .
    .
    <statement-N>
```

In place of a base class name `BaseClassName`, other arbitrary expressions are also allowed. This is useful, for example, when the base class is defined in another module:

```
class DerivedClassName(modname.BaseClassName):
```

The following example demonstrates class inheritance.

```
class Parent:            # Base class definition
    parentAttr=100

    def __init__(self):
        print "Base class"

    def parentMethod(self):
        print 'Base class method'

    def setAttr(self, attr):
        Parent.parentAttr=attr

    def getAttr(self):
        print "Parent attribute :",Parent.parentAttr
```

```
class Child(Parent):    # Derived class definition

    def __init__(self):
        print "Derived class"

    def childMethod(self):
        print 'Derived class method'

c=Child()
c.childMethod()
c.parentMethod()
c.setAttr(200)
c.getAttr()
```

The output is:

```
Derived class
Derived class method
Base class method
Parent attribute : 200
```

Execution of a derived class definition proceeds in the same way as for a base class. If a requested attribute is not found in the class, the search proceeds to look in the base class. This rule is applied recursively, if the base class itself is derived from some other class.

The following example is a step further in understanding inheritance.

```
class Person:
    population=0

    def __init__(self,Name,Age):
        self.name=Name
        self.age=Age
        Person.population+=1

    def Record(self):
        print('Name:"{0}" Age:"{1}"'.format(self.name,self.age))

class Employee(Person):

    def __init__(self,Name,Age,Salary):
        Person.__init__(self,Name,Age)
        self.salary=Salary
        print('Entered record for {0}'.format(self.name))

    def Record(self):
        Person.Record(self)
        print('Salary: "{0:d}"'.format(self.salary))
```

```
class Employer(Person):

    def __init__(self,Name,Age,Percentage):
        Person.__init__(self,Name,Age)
        self.percentage=Percentage
        print('Entered record for {0}'.format(self.name))

    def Record(self):
        Person.Record(self)
        print('Partnership percent: "{0:d}"'.format(self.percentage))

employee1=Employee('Ram',26,25000)
employee2=Employee('Ahmed',20,50000)
employee3=Employee('John',22,75000)
employer1=Employer('Michael',58,60)
employer2=Employer('Kishan',52,40)

members=[employee1,employee2,employee3,employer1,employer2]
for member in members:
    member.Record()
```

The output is:

```
Entered record for Ram
Entered record for Ahmed
Entered record for John
Entered record for Michael
Entered record for Kishan
Name:"Ram" Age:"26"
Salary: "25000"
Name:"Ahmed" Age:"20"
Salary: "50000"
Name:"John" Age:"22"
Salary: "75000"
Name:"Michael" Age:"58"
Partnership percent: "60"
Name:"Kishan" Age:"52"
Partnership percent: "40"
```

Please note that, if a base class has an __init__() method, the derived class's __init__() method, if any, must explicitly call it, to ensure proper initialization of the base class part of the instance; for example: BaseClass.__init__(self,[args...]).

6.2.1. New-style and classic classes
Classes and instances come in two flavors: old-style (or classic) and new-style. New-style classes were introduced in Python 2.2. For compatibility reasons, classes are still old-style by default. Any class which inherits from object is a new-style class. The object class is a base for all new style classes. The following is an example showing simple definitions of old-style and new-style classes.

```
>>> class ClassicExample:
...      def __init__(self):
...         pass
...
>>> class NewStyleExample(object):
...      def __init__(self):
...         pass
...
>>>
```

6.2.2. Overriding Methods

Derived classes may override methods of their base classes. A method of a base class that calls another method defined in the same base class may end up calling a method of a derived class that overrides it.

```
# InheritenceExample2.py

class Parent:            # Base class definition

    def printInfo(self):
        print 'Base class method'

    def parentMethod(self):
        self.printInfo()

class Child(Parent):     # Derived class definition

    def printInfo(self):
        print 'Derived class method'

c=Child()
c.parentMethod()
```

The output is:

```
Derived class method
```

It can be seen that `printInfo()` of derived class is called instead of base class.

6.2.3. Super() function

The is a built-in function `super()`, which can be used for accessing inherited methods that have been overridden in a class. The `super()` only works for new-style classes; in a class hierarchy with single inheritance, super can be used to refer to parent classes without naming them explicitly, thus making the code more maintainable.

```
class Parent(object):    # Base class definition

    def printInfo(self):
```

```
            print 'Base class method'

    def parentMethod(self):
        self.printInfo()

class Child(Parent):      # Derived class definition

    def printInfo(self):
        super(Child,self).printInfo()
#           Parent.printInfo(self)
        print 'Derived class method'


c=Child()
c.parentMethod()
```

The output is:

```
Base class method
Derived class method
```

In the above example, to access the `printInfo()` method of `Parent` class, `super()` method in the form of `super(Child,self).printInfo()` is used, where the name of base class is not mentioned. The other way would have been by using `Parent.printInfo(self)`.

6.2.4. Name mangling

In Python, there is a mechanism called "name mangling" to avoid name clashes of names in class with names defined by sub-classes. Any identifier of the form ___spam (at least two leading underscores, at most one trailing underscore) is textually replaced with _classname___spam, where classname is the current class name. Note that, the mangling rule is designed mostly to avoid accidents.

```
# InheritenceExample3.py

class Parent:              # Base class definition

    def __printInfo(self):
        print 'Base class method'

    def parentMethod(self):
        self.__printInfo()

class Child(Parent):      # Derived class definition

    def __printInfo(self):
        print 'Derived class method'

c=Child()
print Parent.__dict__.keys()
print Child.__dict__.keys()
```

```
c.parentMethod()
c._Child__printInfo()
c._Parent__printInfo()
```

The output is:

```
['__module__', '_Parent__printInfo', '__doc__', 'parentMethod']
['__module__', '__doc__', '_Child__printInfo']
Base class method
Derived class method
Base class method
```

6.2.5.   Multiple inheritence

Till now, the discussion was about inheriting from one class; this is called "single inheritance". Python also supports "multiple inheritance", where a class can inherit from more than one class. A simple class definition inheriting from multiple base classes looks like:

```
class DerivedClassName(Base1,Base2,Base3):
    <statement-1>
    .
    .
    .
    <statement-N>
```

Whenever there is a call via `DerivedClassName` class instance, Python has to look-up the possible function in the class hierarchy for `Base1, Base2 , Base3` ....., but it needs to do this in a consistent order. To do this, Python uses an approach called "method resolution order" (MRO) using an algorithm called "C3" to get it straight.

Consider the following multiple inheritance example.

```
class A(object):
    def printInfo(self):
        print 'Class A'

class B(A):
    def printInfo(self):
        print 'Class B'
#       super(B,self).printInfo()
        A.printInfo(self)

class C(A):
    def printInfo(self):
        print 'Class C'
        super(C,self).printInfo()
class D(B,C):
    def printInfo(self):
        print 'Class D'
```

```
        super(D,self).printInfo()

foo=D()
foo.printInfo()
```

Running the code yield the following output.

```
Class D
Class B
Class A
```

It can be observed that `C` class `printInfo()` is skipped. The reason for that is because `B` class `printInfo()` calls `A` class `printInfo()` directly. The purpose of `super()` is to entertain method resolution order. Now un-comment `super(B,self).printInfo()` and comment-out `A.printInfo(self)`. The code now yields a different result.

```
Class D
Class B
Class C
Class A
```

Now all the `printInfo()` methods get called. Notice that at the time of defining `B.printInfo()`, one can think that `super(B,self).printInfo()` is the same as calling `A.printInfo(self)`, however, this is wrong. In the above situation, `super(B,self).printInfo()` actually calls `C.printInfo(self)`.

Chapter 7
NUMPY

As discussed previously, simple one dimensional array operations can be executed using list, tuple etc. But carrying out multi-dimensional array operations using list is not easy. Python has an `array` module which provides methods for creating array, but they are slower to index than list. A good choice for carrying array operations is by using "NumPy" package.

NumPy is a Python package (licensed under the BSD license) which is helpful in scientific computing by providing multi-dimensional array object, various derived objects (such as masked arrays and matrices), and collection of routines for fast operations on arrays, including mathematical, logical, shape manipulation, sorting, basic linear algebra, basic statistical operations, and many more. At the core of the NumPy package, there is `ndarray` object which encapsulates *n*-dimensional arrays of homogeneous data types. There are several important differences between NumPy array and the standard Python sequence:

- NumPy array has a fixed size at creation, unlike Python list (which can grow dynamically). Changing the size of an `ndarray` will create a new array and delete the original.
- All elements in a NumPy array are required to be of the same data type..
- NumPy array facilitate advanced mathematical and other types of operations on large numbers of data. Typically, such operations are executed more efficiently and with less code than is possible using Python's built-in sequences.

7.1. History

NumPy is built on (and is a successor to) the successful "Numeric" package. Numeric was reasonably complete and stable, remains available, but is now obsolete. Numeric was originally written in 1995 largely by Jim Hugunin, while he was a graduate student at MIT. In 2001, Travis Oliphant along with Eric Jones and Pearu Peterson created "SciPy", which had the the strenght of Numeric package along additional functionality. At about the same time as SciPy was being built, some Numeric users were hitting up against the limited capabilities of Numeric. As a result, "numarray" (now obselete) was created by Perry Greenfield, Todd Miller, and RickWhite at the Space Science Telescope Institute as a replacement for Numeric. In early 2005, Travis Oliphant initiated an effort to bring the diverging community together under a common framework. The effort was paid off with the release of a new package Numpy (with version 0.9.2) in early 2006, which is an amalgam of the code base of Numeric with additional features of numarray. The NumPy name was christened from the unofficial name of "Numerical Python".

7.2. Numpy installation

This section discusses the simple installation approaches of NumPy in different operating system.

7.2.1. Windows

By default, NumPy is not shipped with official Python installer. But one can download (from website link: *http://sourceforge.net/projects/numpy/files/NumPy/*) the executable file of NumPy (recent version 1.8.1) followed by installing it. Before installing NumPy, please make sure that Python is already installed. NumPy is already included in Python(x,y) package, so one does not have to install NumPy separately, if the programmer is using Python(x,y).

7.2.2. Linux

One can install NumPy in Ubuntu (Linux) operating system by executing the following commands in the terminal (as shown in figure 6-1).

```
sudo apt-get install python-numpy
```

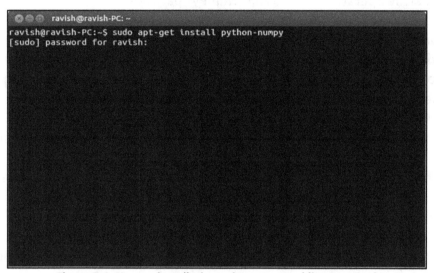

Figure 7-1: Numpy installation using command line terminal

7.3. Data types

Some of the data types supported by NumPy are given in table 6-1.

Table 7-1: Numpy data types

Data type	Description
bool_	Boolean (True or False) stored as a byte.
int8	Byte (ranging from -128 to 127).
int16	Integer (ranging from -32768 to 32767).
int32	Integer (ranging from -2147483648 to 2147483647).
int64	Integer (ranging from -9223372036854775808 to 9223372036854775807).
uint8	Unsigned integer (ranging from 0 to 255).
uint16	Unsigned integer (ranging from 0 to 65535).
uint32	Unsigned integer (ranging from 0 to 4294967295).
uint64	Unsigned integer (ranging from 0 to 18446744073709551615).
float_	Shorthand for float64.
float16	Half precision float: sign bit, 5 bits exponent, 10 bits mantissa.
float32	Single precision float: sign bit, 8 bits exponent, 23 bits mantissa.
float64	Double precision float: sign bit, 11 bits exponent, 52 bits mantissa.
complex_	Shorthand for complex128.
complex64	Complex number, represented by two 32-bit floats (real and imaginary components).
complex128	Complex number, represented by two 64-bit floats (real and imaginary components).

7.4. NumPy array

NumPy's main object is the homogeneous multi-dimensional array. It is a table of elements (usually numbers), all of the same type, indexed by a tuple of positive integers. In NumPy, array dimensions are called "axes", and the number of axes is known as "rank". For example, the coordinates of a point in 3D space [1, 2, 1] is an array of rank 1, because it has one axis and that axis has a length of 3. In the following example, the array has rank 2 (it is two dimensional). The first dimension (axis) has a length of 2, the second dimension has a length of 3.

```
[[ 1., 0., 0.],
 [ 0., 1., 2.]]
```

Some of the attributes of an `ndarray` object are:

`ndarray.ndim`
The number of axes (dimensions) or rank of the array.

`ndarray.shape`
The dimensions of the array. This is a tuple of integers indicating the size of the array in each dimension. For an array of `n` rows and `m` columns, shape will be `(n,m)`. The length of the shape tuple is therefore the rank `ndim`.

`ndarray.size`
The total number of elements of the array. This is equal to the product of the elements of shape.

`ndarray.dtype`
An object describing the type of the elements in the array. One can create or specify `dtype` using standard Python type. Additionally, NumPy provides types of its own, `numpy.int32`, `numpy.int16`, and `numpy.float64` are some examples.

`ndarray.itemsize`
The size in bytes of each element of the array. For example, an array of elements of type `float64` has `itemsize` as 8 (=64/8), while one of type `complex32` has `itemsize` as 4 (=32/8). It is equivalent to `ndarray.dtype.itemsize`.

```
>>> import numpy as np
>>> a=np.array([[ 0,  1,  2,  3,  4],
...             [ 5,  6,  7,  8,  9],
...             [10, 11, 12, 13, 14]])
>>> type(a)
<type 'numpy.ndarray'>
>>> a.shape
(3, 5)
>>> a.ndim
2
>>> a.dtype
dtype('int32')
```

```
>>> a.dtype.name
'int32'
>>> a.itemsize
4
>>> a.size
15
```

7.4.1. Array creation

There are several ways to create NumPy array, one approach is from a regular Python list or tuple using the `array()` method. The type of the resulting array is deduced from the type of the elements in the sequences.

```
>>> import numpy as np
>>> a=np.array([1,2,3])
>>> a.dtype
dtype('int32')
>>> b=np.array((1.2,3.4,5.6))
>>> b.dtype
dtype('float64')
```

A frequent error consists in calling `array()` with multiple numeric arguments, rather than providing a single list or tuple of numbers as an argument.

```
>>> a=np.array(1,2,3,4)      # WRONG
>>> a=np.array([1,2,3,4])    # RIGHT
```

`array()` transforms sequence of sequences into two-dimensional arrays, sequences of sequences of sequences into three-dimensional arrays, and so on.

```
>>> b=np.array([(1.5,2,3),(4,5,6)])
>>> b
array([[ 1.5,  2. ,  3. ],
       [ 4. ,  5. ,  6. ]])
```

The type of the array can also be explicitly specified at creation time:

```
>>> c=np.array([[1,2],[3,4]],dtype=np.complex)
>>> c
array([[ 1.+0.j,  2.+0.j],
       [ 3.+0.j,  4.+0.j]])
```

Often the elements of an array are initially unknown, but array size is known. Hence, NumPy offers several functions to create array with initial placeholder content. The function `zeros()` create an array full of zeros, the function `ones()` create an array full of ones, and the function `empty()` create an array whose initial content is random. By default, the `dtype` of the created array is `float64`.

```
>>> np.zeros((3,4))
array([[ 0.,  0.,  0.,  0.],
```

```
       [ 0.,   0.,   0.,   0.],
       [ 0.,   0.,   0.,   0.]])
>>> np.zeros([3,4])
array([[ 0.,   0.,   0.,   0.],
       [ 0.,   0.,   0.,   0.],
       [ 0.,   0.,   0.,   0.]])
>>> np.ones((2,3,4),dtype=np.int16)
array([[[1, 1, 1, 1],
        [1, 1, 1, 1],
        [1, 1, 1, 1]],

       [[1, 1, 1, 1],
        [1, 1, 1, 1],
        [1, 1, 1, 1]]], dtype=int16)
>>> np.empty((2,3))
array([[  1.39069238e-309,   1.39069238e-309,   1.39069238e-309],
       [  1.39069238e-309,   1.39069238e-309,   1.39069238e-309]])
```

To create sequences of numbers, NumPy provides a function `arange()`, analogous to Python's built-in function `range()`, that returns array instead of list.

```
>>> np.arange(10,30,5)
array([10, 15, 20, 25])
>>> np.arange(0,2,0.3)
array([ 0. ,  0.3,  0.6,  0.9,  1.2,  1.5,  1.8])
```

When `arange()` is used with floating point arguments, it is generally not possible to predict the number of elements obtained, due to the finite floating point precision. For this reason, it is usually better to use the function `linspace()`, that receives as an argument the number of elements that we want, instead of the step:

```
>>> np.linspace(0,2,5)
array([ 0. ,  0.5,  1. ,  1.5,  2. ])
>>> np.linspace(0,np.pi,4)
array([ 0.        ,  1.04719755,  2.0943951 ,  3.14159265])
```

7.4.2. Printing array
While printing an array, NumPy display it in a similar way to nested lists, but with the following layout:
- the last axis is printed from left to right.
- the second-to-last is printed from top to bottom.
- the rest are also printed from top to bottom, with each slice separated from the next by an empty line.

```
>>> np.arange(6)                    # 1d array
array([0, 1, 2, 3, 4, 5])
>>>
>>> np.arange(12).reshape(4,3)      # 2d array
array([[ 0,  1,  2],
```

```
          [ 3,   4,   5],
          [ 6,   7,   8],
          [ 9, 10, 11]])
>>>
>>> np.arange(24).reshape(2,3,4)          # 3d array
array([[[ 0,   1,   2,   3],
          [ 4,   5,   6,   7],
          [ 8,   9, 10, 11]],

         [[12, 13, 14, 15],
          [16, 17, 18, 19],
          [20, 21, 22, 23]]])
```

If an array is too large to be printed, NumPy automatically skips the central part of the array and only print the corners:

```
>>> np.arange(10000)
array([    0,    1,    2, ...,  9997, 9998, 9999])
>>>
>>> np.arange(10000).reshape(100,100)
array([[    0,    1,    2, ...,   97,   98,   99],
         [  100,  101,  102, ...,  197,  198,  199],
         [  200,  201,  202, ...,  297,  298,  299],
         ...,
         [9700, 9701, 9702, ..., 9797, 9798, 9799],
         [9800, 9801, 9802, ..., 9897, 9898, 9899],
         [9900, 9901, 9902, ..., 9997, 9998, 9999]])
```

To disable this behaviour and force NumPy to print the entire array, the printing option `set_printoptions` need to be changed.

```
>>> np.set_printoptions(threshold='nan')
```

7.5. Basic Operations

Arithmetic operations when applied on NumPy arrays, they are implemented element-wise.

```
>>> a=np.array([20,30,40,50])
>>> b=np.arange(4)
>>> c=a-b
>>> c
array([20, 29, 38, 47])
>>> b**2
array([0, 1, 4, 9])
>>> a<39
array([ True,  True, False, False], dtype=bool)
```

The product operator * operates element-wise in NumPy arrays. The matrix product can be performed using the `dot()` function or creating matrix objects (refer section 7.8).

```
>>> a=np.array([[1,1],
...             [0,1]])
>>> b=np.array([[2,0],
...             [3,4]])
>>> a*b
array([[2, 0],
       [0, 4]])
>>> np.dot(a,b)
array([[5, 4],
       [3, 4]])
```

Some operations, such as +=, *=, etc., modifies an existing array, rather than creating a new array.

```
>>> a=np.array([[1,2],          # a is integer type
...             [3,4]])
>>> b=np.array([[1.,2.],        # b is float type
...             [3.,4.]])
>>> a*=2
>>> a
array([[2, 4],
       [6, 8]])
>>> b+=a
>>> b
array([[  3.,   6.],
       [  9.,  12.]])
>>> a+=b                        # b is converted to integer type
>>> a
array([[ 5, 10],
       [15, 20]])
```

When operating with arrays of different types, the type of the resulting array corresponds to the more general or precise one (a behavior known as "upcasting").

```
>>> a=np.array([1.1,2.2,3.3])
>>> a.dtype.name
'float64'
>>> b=np.array([4,5,6])
>>> b.dtype.name
'int32'
>>> c=a+b
>>> c
array([ 5.1,  7.2,  9.3])
>>> c.dtype.name
'float64'
```

Many unary operations, such as computing the sum of all the elements in the array, are implemented as methods of the ndarray class .

[167]

```
>>> a=np.array([[5,8],
...             [3,6]])
>>> a.sum()
22
>>> a.min()
3
>>> a.max()
8
```

By default, these operations apply to the array as though it were a list of numbers, regardless of its shape. However, by specifying the axis parameter you can apply an operation along the specified axis of an array:

```
>>> a=np.arange(12).reshape(3,4)
>>> a
array([[ 0,  1,  2,  3],
       [ 4,  5,  6,  7],
       [ 8,  9, 10, 11]])
>>> a.sum(axis=0)              # Sum of each column
array([12, 15, 18, 21])
>>> a.min(axis=1)             # Minimum of each row
array([0, 4, 8])
>>> a.cumsum(axis=1)          # Cumulative sum along each row
array([[ 0,  1,  3,  6],
       [ 4,  9, 15, 22],
       [ 8, 17, 27, 38]])
```

7.6. Universal functions

NumPy provides familiar mathematical functions such as `sin()`, `cos()`, `exp()`, etc. In NumPy, these are called "universal functions". Within NumPy, these functions operate element-wise on an array, producing an array as output.

```
>>> a=np.arange(3)
>>> a
array([0, 1, 2])
>>> np.exp(a)
array([ 1.       ,  2.71828183,  7.3890561 ])
>>> np.sqrt(a)
array([ 0.       ,  1.       ,  1.41421356])
```

7.7. Copying array

When operating and manipulating arrays, their elements sometimes needs to be copied into a new array, and sometimes not. This is often a source of confusion for beginners. Simple assignment does not make copy of array data.

```
>>> a=np.arange(12)
>>> b=a
>>> id(a)
```

```
85660040
>>> id(b)
85660040
>>> b is a       # a and b are two names for the same ndarray object
True
```

Python passes mutable objects as references, so function calls make no copy.

```
>>> def F(x):
...      print id(x)
...
>>> id(a)
85660040
>>> F(a)
85660040
```

The `copy` method makes a complete copy of the array data.

```
>>> c=a.copy()
>>> c
array([ 0,  1,  2,  3,  4,  5,  6,  7,  8,  9, 10, 11])
>>> c is a
False
>>> c[0]=999
>>> c
array([999,   1,   2,   3,   4,   5,   6,   7,   8,   9,  10,  11])
>>> a
array([ 0,  1,  2,  3,  4,  5,  6,  7,  8,  9, 10, 11])
```

7.8. The Matrix Class

There is also a `matrix` class, which returns a matrix from an array-like object, or from a string of data. A matrix is a specialized 2-D array that retains its 2-D nature through operations.

```
>>> np.matrix([[1.0,2.0],[3.0,4.0]])
matrix([[ 1.,  2.],
        [ 3.,  4.]])
>>> a=np.matrix('1.0 2.0;3.0 4.0')
>>> a
matrix([[ 1.,  2.],
        [ 3.,  4.]])
>>> a.T                        # Transpose of a matrix
matrix([[ 1.,  3.],
        [ 2.,  4.]])
>>> x=np.matrix('5.0 7.0')
>>> y=x.T
>>> y
matrix([[ 5.],
        [ 7.]])
>>> a*y                        # Matrix multiplication
```

```
matrix([[ 19.],
        [ 43.]])
>>> a.I                          # Inverse of a matrix
matrix([[-2. ,   1. ],
        [ 1.5, -0.5]])
```

Chapter 8
FILE HANDLING

There are several ways to present the output of a program; data can be printed on computer monitor in a human-readable form, or written to a file (for example, image.jpg, notes.txt, etc.) for future use. A computer file (or simply "file") is a resource for storing information, which is available to a computer program, and is usually based on some kind of durable electronic storage. A file is durable in the sense that it remains available for programs to use after the current program has finished. Computer file can be considered as the modern counterpart of paper document which traditionally are kept in office files, library files, etc., and this is the source of the term.

8.1. File opening

A common operation needed during program execution is to load data from an existing file or to create a new file to store data. To accomplish this, the program first needs to open a file, which is executed using `open()` function. The `open()` returns a file object, and is most commonly used with two arguments, `filename` and `mode`.

The first argument is a string containing the filename. The second argument is another string containing a few characters describing the way in which the file will be used. `mode` can be `'r'` when the file will only be read, `'w'` for only writing (an existing file with the same name will be erased), and `'a'` opens the file for appending, any data written to the file is automatically added to the end. The `mode` argument is optional,with `'r'` as default. Modes `'r+'`, `'w+'` and `'a+'` opens the file for both for updating (note that `'w+'` truncates the file).

Windows operating system makes a distinction between text and binary files, so in Windows, `'b'` appended to the `mode` opens the file in binary mode, therefore, there are also modes like `'rb'`, `'wb'`, and `'r+b'`.

To understand the various methods which are helpful in reading information from the file, a text file is manually created (having empty line after every text line) having filename *list.txt*, and kept at path *C:/test*. The content of the file is:

```
This is first line.

This is second line.

This is third line.

This is fourth and last line.
```

Now, open the file using `open()` function in read mode.

```
>>> f=open('C:/test/list.txt','r')
```

8.2. Reading file

To read a file's contents, call `read(size)` method, which read `size` bytes of data and returns it as a string. `size` is an optional numeric argument. When `size` is omitted or negative, the entire contents of the file will be read and returned; otherwise, at most `size` bytes are read and returned. If the end of the file has been reached, `read()` will return an empty string (' ').

```
>>> f.read(19)
'This is first line.'
```

There is a `tell()` method, which returns an integer giving the file object's current position in the file, measured in bytes from the beginning of the file.

```
>>> f.tell()
19L
```

To change the file object's position, use `seek(offset, from_what)` method. The position is computed from adding `offset` to a reference point; the reference point is selected by the `from_what` argument. A `from_what` value of 0 measures from the beginning of the file, 1 uses the current file position, and 2 uses the end of the file as the reference point. `from_what` can be omitted and defaults to 0, using the beginning of the file as the reference point.

```
>>> f.seek(-52,2)
>>> f.read()
'This is third line.\n\nThis is fourth and last line.'
>>> f.tell()
99L
>>> f.seek(0,0)
>>> f.tell()
0L
>>> f.read()
'This is first line.\n\nThis is second line.\n\nThis is third
line.\n\nThis is fourth and last line.'
```

When relevant operations on a file are finished, use `close()` method to close the file and free-up any system resources taken up by the open file. After calling `close()`, attempt to use the file object will automatically fail.

```
>>> f.close()
>>> f.read()
Traceback (most recent call last):
  File "<stdin>", line 1, in ?
ValueError: I/O operation on closed file
```

There is also a `readline()` method that read a single line from the file; a newline character (\n) is left at the end of the string, and is only omitted on the last line of the file, if the file does not end in a newline. If `readline()` returns an empty string, the end of the file has been reached, while a blank line is represented by '\n'.

```
>>> f=open('C:/test/list.txt','r')
>>> f.readline()
'This is first line.\n'
>>> f.readline()
'\n'
>>> f.readline()
'This is second line.\n'
>>> f.readline()
'\n'
>>> f.readline()
'This is third line.\n'
>>> f.readline()
'\n'
>>> f.readline()
'This is fourth and last line.'
>>> f.readline()
''
>>> f.close()
```

For reading lines from a file, one can also loop over the file object. This is memory efficient, fast, and leads to simple code:

```
>>> f=open('C:/test/list.txt','r')
>>> for line in f:
...      print line,
...
This is first line.

This is second line.

This is third line.

This is fourth and last line.
>>> f.close()
```

If there is a requirement to read all lines of a file in a list, one can do `list(f)` or `f.readlines()`.

```
>>> f=open('C:/test/list.txt','r')
>>> list(f)
['This is first line.\n', '\n', 'This is second line.\n', '\n', 'This
is third line.\n', '\n', 'This is fourth and last line.']
>>> f.close()
>>>
>>> f=open('C:/test/list.txt','r')
>>> f.readlines()
['This is first line.\n', '\n', 'This is second line.\n', '\n', 'This
is third line.\n', '\n', 'This is fourth and last line.']
>>> f.close()
```

8.3. Writing to a file

Apart from only reading information from a file, there can be a scenario where some data need to be written to a file. To carry out such operation, `write(string)` method is used, where `string` argument should be of string data type. Upon success, `write()` method returns `None`.

Open "list.txt" and add some text at the end of the file.

```
>>> f=open('C:/test/list.txt','a+')
>>> f.write('\n\nThis is the new last line.')
>>> f.seek(0,0)
>>> f.read()
'This   is   first   line.\n\nThis   is   second   line.\n\nThis   is   third
line.\n\nThis is fourth and last line.\n\nThis is the new last line.'
>>> f.close()
```

8.4. File renaming and deletion

Python's `os` module provide methods for renaming and deleting files. To rename a file, use `rename(src,dst)` method, where `src` argument is source filename, while `dst` is destination filename.

```
>>> import os
>>> os.rename('C:/test/list.txt','C:/test/newlist.txt')
```

To delete a file, use remove() method.

```
>>> os.remove('C:/test/newlist.txt')
```